# Tenbury
### and the
# Teme Valley

# People and Places

# Tenbury
### and the
# Teme Valley

# People and Places

*by*
### Tenbury & District
### Civic & Historical Society

*compiled by*
### W. Hayes

### Logaston Press

LOGASTON PRESS
Little Logaston Woonton Almeley
Herefordshire HR3 6QH
logastonpress.co.uk


First published by Logaston Press 2007
Copyright © Tenbury & District Civic & Historical Society 2007

ISBN 978 1904396 83 3


Typeset by Logaston Press
and printed in Great Britain by
Bell and Bain Ltd., Glasgow

# Contents

# Howard Miller 1929–2005

This is Howard Miller's book — the one he did not have time to write.

The Tenbury & District Civic & Historical Society will be eternally grateful for the donation of Howard's extensive notes and archives by his wife, Mary. His huge collection has been the basis for this book.

Howard was dedicated to understanding the uniqueness of the town and area. His files contain notes and stories about the unusual, the funny, the terrible, the victorious and the very poignant events occurring in Tenbury and the Teme Valley from early days to modern times.

He loved Tenbury and, with thanks, this book is dedicated to him.

# Acknowledgements

I am eternally grateful for the research and writing, encouragement, wise counsel and support that interested members of the Society have given me in the production of the book you now hold.

In particular: Peter Bevis and John Asquith for all the writing and research that they undertook, sometimes at short notice; Patrick Shaw and Derek Marks for taking on subjects that they researched and wrote up with such enthusiasm; Chris Trouteau for the hours of cataloguing audio tapes; Betty Boffey for much detailed knowledge about Tenbury and the Spilsbury family for a glimpse into a treasured memoir of their family. Special thanks are also due to Val Greenhill for her generous proof reading and helpful comments, David Hambelton for his considerable photographic skills and to Andrew Ferrier, Geoff Mytton, Frank Crisp, Tom Dallow and Mrs A. Thompson for additional research and information. I am also grateful to the Governors of Goffs Primary School in Gorsley for permission to use the drawing on p.34 and Brian Woodruffe for permission to use the photo of the Hardman window of the rear cover.

I acknowledge my sincere debt to you all and hope that you are pleased with the result.

W. Hayes

# Please note

We have made all attempts possible to locate the copyright holders of material used, but because much of the material from which these articles originated was in the form of handwritten notes and a great deal is unattributed, we apologise for any errors or omissions of acknowledgement.

Some chapters are taken from personal recollections and personal archives. As such they are personal interpretations of events and times. We did not feel that we could interfere with these, but quote them in the spirit in which they were written. There may therefore be errors of fact or interpretation.

It would be very helpful if we could be notified of mistakes or omissions so that the reference might be researched further and corrections made in future editions. Please send any information that might help us to: The Secretary, Tenbury and District Civic and Historical Society, Bramleigh, St. Mary's Close, Tenbury Wells, Worcs. WR15 8ES.

W. Hayes

# Augustine's Oak at Abberley

Initially a very small and vulnerable sect, the Christian religion was established in England before the end of the Roman era. In 313 AD the Roman Emperor Constantine II legalised Christianity and in 324 made it the official religion of the Roman Empire. However, by the beginning of the 7th century, the Celtic Church, because of its isolation, had diverged in some practices from the official Church in Rome.

A few years earlier, in 597, Pope Gregory sent Augustine with 40 monks and numerous adherents to England to restore the Church of Rome and where possible to baptise heathens into the ways of the One True Church. Augustine is known as the saint who prayed as a young man for chastity, 'but not yet'. Augustine began his mission in Kent with the successful conversion of King Ethelbert whose Queen, Bertha, was a Frankish Christian princess. His assistants also made progress in Essex and Northumbria.

Augustine was allowed to make certain compromises with Saxon customs in order to ensure the success of his mission, even to the point of consecrating heathen temples for Christian uses. It is probably due to this that some of our existing churches have Celtic or pagan roots, many being built on sites of pagan worship. Others retain sculpture or structures with pagan heritage. Examples can be found in the many Norman churches in the Teme Valley.

Recognising that there were several Celtic bishops in Britain, each with his own priorities and ways of interpreting the Christian calendar, Pope Gregory ordered Augustine to convene a meeting to agree a single calendar. However, the Celtic bishops were reluctant to change to suit the Roman Christians. It is fairly certain that the meeting took place in 602, but there has since been much debate as to where it took place. Records differ, of course, but it seems that the British bishops of mid, south and north Wales attended the meeting, as did the Abbot of Bangor and seven other bishops from the area of Caerleon.

The Venerable Bede refers to the meeting place as 'on the borders of the Hwiccii', a Saxon people who then occupied part of what is now Worcestershire. Some historians have interpreted the site as being at Rock or Abberley on the north-western borders of Hwiccian territory.

*Augustine's Oak at Abberley in 2007*

This could be correct as there are known Roman camps and roadways between Worcester and Abberley, providing easy access from the east. In addition, as much travel was then by river, Abberley, lying close to both Severn and Teme, would have made it easy for the Celtic bishops to attend. Other evidence in support of this theory is that Rock in Saxon records was probably known as *Thaer Ac* meaning oak; that in Domesday it was called *Halac* which may mean Holy Oak; and that the settlement of Abberley was founded in Saxon times in the parish now known as Rock.

To ensure that the meeting even took place required some sympathetic negotiation, but the King of Kent, Ethelbert, where Augustine had begun his ministry, had a son Eadbald who had very good relations with the Celtic Welsh. Eadbald may well have given his name to the hill that he and his entourage occupied during the conferences and to the settlement of Abberley itself.

It may seem odd to hold such an important conference under an oak, but structures capable of holding a large number of people were rare. Trees like oak or yew provided reasonable shelter and were large enough and distinctive enough to be easily located. Because of this use, they were often known as Apostles' Oaks, Mitre Oaks, Christ's Oaks or Gospel Oaks. However, the tree at Abberley has always been known as Augustine's Oak and this would suggest that it is a good candidate for the site of the meeting.

The first meeting failed amidst much bad feeling and without any resolution. A second meeting was organised and prior to it the Celtic bishops consulted a hermit who advised them to place a chair under an oak and to 'ask Augustine to sit there with his followers'. As the bishops approached they were to note what Augustine did. 'If he rises to greet you, do as he says, as this will show him to be a humble man and a true follower of Christ. If Augustine does not rise, do not do as he says, as this shows him to be a proud and unfeeling man.'

According to the story, Augustine did not rise from the chair and the Celtic churches continued to celebrate Easter according to the old calendar for a further 200 years.

Augustine died not long after – in 604 – and almost immediately much of the work that he had done to convert England to Christianity was undone by tribal revolts and the resurgence of paganism. However there was optimism for the religion in the north-east. Ethelberga, the daughter of King Ethelbert and Bertha, married Edwin, the King of Northumbria, and converted him to Christianity in 627. In 635 the monastery at Lindisfarne was founded and the Synod of Whitby was convened in 664 to discuss the differences that Augustine failed to reconcile. It was decided to follow the Roman rules and thus, over time, the Christians of Britain were united with those in the rest of Europe.

As for the oak? Not having the longevity of yews, the oak will have died centuries ago, but it and its successors were marked on maps for ever after. A very large and very old oak was on the site in 1753 when the turnpike road went past it. Being hollow it was fitted with a seat and a thatched roof for the shelter of the turnpike keeper. Sadly, when he lit a fire all was burnt. A sapling was planted but mistakenly cut down. A mature tree presently stands near the site, which had been marked by a stone, and a sapling was planted in 2000 to ensure a continuing Augustine's Oak.

# Burford Church and the Cornewalls

A church was recorded at Burford in the Domesday Book. It was much smaller than the present church, with a chancel and nave, but was extended over the centuries and eventually served as the mother church for Boraston, Nash, Whitton, and possibly Greete, until 1849.

The north and south walls of the present chancel were part of the original structure, but the east wall was demolished in the 14th century, to allow for a decorated window to be installed.

In 1304, at the age of 8, Margaret Mortimer of Wigmore Castle and heir to the Burford Estate, married Sir Geoffrey Cornewall. Sir Geoffrey was the great grandson of King John and became the first Cornewall to hold the Burford Estate. The most important of the Cornewalls, however, was John, Sir

*An aerial photograph showing the relationship of the church to Burford House*

5

Geoffrey's grandson. John married Princess Elizabeth, the daughter of John of Gaunt and sister of Henry IV.

Elizabeth Plantagenet of Lancaster had been married twice before. Her first marriage was to John Hastings, Earl of Pembroke, and took place at Kenilworth Castle on 24 June 1380. He was just 8 years old and she was 16. The marriage was annulled in 1382 and John Hastings died in 1389. Her second marriage was to John Holland, the Earl of Huntingdon, in 1384. This marriage failed because her new husband was convicted of involvement in a conspiracy to murder her father, John of Gaunt, and her brother, the King. The Earl was executed and Elizabeth later married Sir John Cornewall. Sir John had been very successful in a tournament at York and went on to distinguish himself at the Battle of Agincourt in 1415. When Elizabeth died in 1425 or 1426, John brought the princess's body to Burford where she lies in a painted tomb in the north of the chancel, ermine and purple signifying her Royal status.

Ten years later, the heart tomb of Edmund, heir to the 5th Baron Cornewall, was placed in the south of the chancel. Because he was guilty of killing two men, he undertook a pilgrimage to the Holy Land to be absolved of his sins. Unfortunately, on his return journey he was killed at Cologne. Before he died, however, he instructed his servant to return his heart to Burford.

Edmund's son, Thomas, became the 6th Baron and fought for the Lancastrians in the Battle of Mortimer's Cross in 1461. The Yorkists won the day and subsequently – once the victor of Mortimer's Cross was crowned Edward IV – the Burford estates were confiscated and awarded to his brother-in-law, Richard Croft of Croft Castle, who had supported the Yorkist cause.

*Burford church*

Thomas was imprisoned in Ludlow Castle, where Richard Croft was the governor and Thomas' sister, Eleanor, the governess. He was released in 1467 and died in 1473.

On the death of Thomas, his son applied to have the manor restored, on the grounds that the son should not have to suffer for the sins of the father. Parliament agreed and he became the 7th Baron.

The tomb of the heir to the 8th Baron lies in a prime position in the centre of the chancel. He died in 1508 at the age of 20, having achieved the status of a champion tilter. His head rests on his own helmet and his feet rest on the suitably crowned ducal lion, the emblem on the shield of the Cornewall family.

In the church is a triptych of 1588 that contains paintings of the 9th Baron, his wife and their son – the 10th Baron, who at 7 feet 3 inches was known as the Giant of Burford. The Giant can also be seen below the main painting, prostrate in his burial shroud, at his true height.

There are also monuments to the 12th and 13th Barons on the south wall of the chancel, showing them at prayer, facing each other. These monuments were erected by the 13th Baron six years before his own death in 1636.

In 1727 the Burford estate was sold to William Bowles, a glassmaker from Wanstead in Essex. The estate passed to the Rushouts by marriage in 1803,

*The triptych in Burford church*

the Rev. Rushout adopting the name of Bowles when he became Lord of the Manor in 1817. In 1842 the Rev. Rushout Bowles died and his son Captain George Rushout became Lord of the Manor. Captain Rushout invited his lifelong friend Rev. Joyce to be rector when he became 3rd Lord Northwick in 1859. Interestingly Captain Rushout and Rev. Joyce died within two days of each other in 1887.

Captain George's sister, Georgina, lived at Burford House all her life and on inheriting the manor, set about having the church restored in memory of her brother. She engaged Sir Aston Webb to supervise the fine work on the oak ceiling (which shows a choir of angels), the altar, reredos, chancel screen and pulpit, and left the church as we see it today. He was considered one of the finest craftsmen of the time.

The church contains some attractive funeral hatchments (heraldic insignia painted on wood or canvas, created on a person's death). The hatchments probably hung in the manor house for six months or so before being brought into the church. They are to the Rev. Rushout Bowles, his wife and Lord & Lady Northwick. The latter hatchment was made during Lady Northwick's lifetime as her coat of arms is on a white background.

The church also has a parish chest showing three locks. One key was given to the rector and the others to the two churchwardens. The chest held the parish registers and on the last service on each Sunday the key holders unlocked it to enable the registers to be updated by the scribe. The Burford registers date back to 1558.

The south door bears the date of 1696 hidden within the studs, whilst the church has five bells.

*The date of 1696 set out in studs in the church door*

# St Mary's Church

Tenbury's Church of St Mary's lies quietly on a grass plinth beside the River Teme. Frequently in need of restoration following flooding, it nevertheless has ancient origins, being listed in the Domesday Book and housing part of a 9th-century preaching cross which was found on the site. Today it consists of a Norman tower, which may have stood apart from the church originally; a nave with three 14th-century window jambs and arches that survived a flood of 1770; and south and north aisles. Because of a later flood, only two 14th-century windows on the south side remain in the 19th-century restorations. An organ chamber and vestry were added in 1865, when the organ was moved from the western gallery where it had been housed since 1843.

*St Mary's church*

In spite of so many recent renovations and rebuildings, St Mary's is both beautiful and unusual. One of its rareties is an Easter Sepulchre, used in medieval times to celebrate the events of Easter, built into the north wall of the chancel, close to the altar. It dates from the 14th century and was used until the Reformation in the mid-16th century. It was on this sepulchre, probably in a simple framework of wood decorated with crimson hangings, that the bread and wine used in the communion service was placed on Good Friday until early on Easter Day. In some churches the Sepulchre was elaborately carved with figures of sleeping Roman soldiers below the shelf and a representation of the Resurrection above. The Sepulchre may also have held a wooden crucifix or statue used for the Easter ceremony. A continual watch was kept in anticipation of the final appearance of Christ. The watchers were supplied with coals, water, ale and candles paid for by donations to cover the annual cost.

*The Easter Sepulchre*

This was a favourite object of devotion in many parishes. Members of the church made bequests to construct, maintain and light the sepulchre. To pay for a taper, the church in Wymynswold (now known as Womenswold, near Canterbury, Kent) was left a cow 'that one within the parish shall ever have to farm and the profit of the cow, so that he maintain a taper of 4 lbs of wax at the least yearly to the honour of the Holy Resurrection of Our Lord'. In Northamptonshire, Thomas Hunt bequeathed ten ewes, another gave ten bee hives. In 1370 a guild was formed in a parish in London to maintain 13 wax lights at one Sepulchre.

St Mary's Church also has one remaining Lenten hook. There would have been two of these to take a Lenten veil across the chancel to hide the altar from public view. Very few of these hooks now remain. The origin of the practice of screening the altar is contained in the Old Testament '... he brought the ark into the tabernacle and set up the curtain for screening and screened the ark of the covenant, as the Lord had commanded Moses.' (Exodus 11:21) A similar procedure takes place in the church today, when the altar is stripped of decorative materials during Lent.

St Mary's Tenbury also has a squint – a rectangular aperture – above the Easter Sepulchre. There used to be an upper room for a priest behind the north wall of the chancel, probably removed when the vestry was built in the 19th century, and the squint allowed the priest a view of the altar.

The Easter Sepulchre, the squint and the hook for the Lenten Veil are reminders of the ceremonies that took place in St Mary's Tenbury during medieval times and are related to the celebration of Easter in the church today. Other examples are found in churches in counties in the north midlands, but the one here is the only known example of this quality in the west.


## The Monuments

### The Cross-legged Knight
A letter in *The Gentleman's Magazine* in 1824 notes that:

> A Gentleman has recovered a specimen of Tomb Architecture, a small figure of a cross legged knight which has been concealed from public view. It has now, by the careful assistance of Mr Thomas Mills, a stonemason, been so far recovered from a whitewash of perhaps two centuries, that every part of the figure that remains is visible. It is so exquisite in workmanship that even the folds produced by the weight of the chain armour are distinctly seen.

A separate letter states:

> The cross legged knight required three men for as many days to take off his Great Coat. If you have time when in Tenbury, give the sexton a shilling to show it to you and if you don't say it is the most exquisite piece of carvery you ever saw, I will give you your shilling again.

However, that would be difficult as the writer did not give a name and address!

Since the figure is so small and holds a heart to his chest, it may commemorate a 13th-century knight whose heart was returned home for burial, a not uncommon practice of the time. It has been placed on the Easter Sepulchre for convenience and it is not known where the heart is buried.

Late in the 12th century, Hugh de Say gave the advowson of Tenbury, Rochford and Leysters to the abbey of Lyra in Normandy. He was later killed in the wars in Wales and it is possible that this small figure may be his effigy.

## The Knight Templar

This figure was described by Major Symonds in his 1645 diary as:

> A Statue of rude bigness, about seven feet long, his shield whereon his arms are carved is at least two foot long. Recumbent figure of Knight Templar, his feet resting on some animal. The right hand grasps the hilt of the sword, the left the scabbard below.

It was damaged during the flood of 1770 when the roof fell on it and broke the legs off below the knee. This monument is probably of a Sturmey of Sutton, who distinguished his zeal in the recovery of the Holy Land.

## The Acton Tomb

Habington's 16th-century manuscripts say of this tomb '... by hym in seemly attire is the resemblence of hys wife, and at her feete a hound.'

This is the alabaster tomb of Thomas and Mary Acton of Sutton Park. In 1543, Andrews and Temple, dealers in churches after the Reformation, conveyed the living of Tenbury cum Rochford and Leysters to Thomas Acton Esq. It remained in the Acton family until 1713. Thomas Acton died on 20 January 1546, aged 70, and Mary his wife, née Lacon, died on 28 April 1564, aged 58. Their two sons, Launcelot and Gabriel, died in their infancy and are commemorated by skulls on the tomb, but their daughter, Joyce, married, at 12, Sir Thomas Lucy of Charlecote, who reputedly prosecuted Shakespeare for deer stealing.

The coat of arms bears those of Acton (a helmet with sword piercing a boar's head) and of Lacon (a sparrow hawk with bells).

Joyce had the tomb erected in 1581 in her parents' memory. It is an excellent representation of dress and fashion of the period and the quality of the carving is remarkable (that of the petticoats is exquisite).

## The Bells

> The bells they sound on Bredon
> And still the steeples hum.
> 'Come all to church good people.'
> Oh, noisy bells be dumb;
> I hear you, I will come.
> (From *A Shropshire Lad* by A.E. Housman)

A set of six bells hangs in the tower at the west end of St Mary's Church in Tenbury, and the bells are marked as follows:

1. 'Come away make no delay' 1787 T. Creswell. 4.1 cwt 26½" diameter (Mr Creswell was a churchwarden)
2. 'Peace and Good neighbourhood' AR 1720. 4.2 cwt 27" diam. (Abel Rhudhall, Gloucester bellfounder)
3. Mr Richard Smith Junior – Sidesman. 2 cwt 28" diam
4. John Gent and John Ward – Churchwardens. 5.3 cwt 29" diam
5. Mr William Read – Vicar 1718-1755. 7.3 cwt 31½" diam.
6. Francis Cornwall – Benefactor 1720 10 cwt 35½" diam

The tombstone of John Gent, remembered on Bell 4, still stands in the churchyard.

The original ring of bells was the last five, all cast by Abel Rhudhall with similar chasing. The first bell, the treble, is still tolled by the clergy each day before morning prayer. In the tower of St Mary's is a copy of the rules for ringers dating back to Victorian times.

Although the tower was built in the 12th century in the Norman style, the top section was added, probably when the church was rebuilt in 1777, to increase the height of the bells so that they could be heard across the town. (In an age when there were few clocks, the bells were essential in getting parishioners to church on time.)

Church bells came to Europe soon after the arrival of Christianity; St Gregory of Tours refers to the bells hanging in towers and sounded by a rope attached to a clapper. Ringing is now carried on in over 5,000 towers throughout the British Isles.

Bells are not just rung to announce church services, but also for celebrations such as weddings and for national celebrations such as, recently, the Queen Mother's 100th birthday. Occasionally, they are rung for funerals and on Remembrance Sunday they are rung half-muffled. The New Year is often associated with the ringing of bells, as expressed in Tennyson's *In Memoriam* 'Ring out the Old, Ring in the New'.

People would often sponsor the bell ringing and in the 1727 the following is recorded:

| | |
|---|---|
| on ye King's Proclamation | 5s 0d |
| 20th October | 5s 0d |
| 5th November | 6s 6d |
| Queen's Birthday | 7s 0d |
| 20th May | 3s 6d |
| King's Accession | 4s 6d |
| King's Proclamation | 5s 0d |

There were expenses of course and in the same year the following payments are noted:

| Wm Pearce | for mending ye bell wheels | 7s 0d |
| | For mending ye bell-free [belfry] steps | 0s 6d |
| | A key for ye bell-free [belfry] | 0s 4d |

The provision of bell ropes was a continuing expense and was at one time paid for with rent from a piece of land on the Oldwood Road called 'Bellacre'.

A plaque on the wall of the church by the west door states 'In 1979 the ring of six bells was restored by John Taylor and Co. of the Bell Foundry, Loughborough, through the generosity of Arthur Handley, late of Gilmorton, Tenbury Wells.'

The current team of bell ringers are all members of the Hereford Diocesan Guild of Bellringers. Visiting ringers often remark how fortunate St Mary's Tenbury Wells is to have such a lovely ring of six bells.

# Skirmish at Bleathwood

The Civil War began after many years of dispute between Charles I and Parliament over various domestic, religious and foreign policy matters. In anger for its lack of co-operation, the King refused to call Parliament between 1629 and 1640 and ruled alone, but lack of money forced a recall of Parliament in order to raise further taxes. This it refused to do without concessions from the King. Both sides started to stockpile arms and in August 1642 the King raised his standard in Nottingham.

Most of the landowners in the Marches were sympathetic to the King and the towns of Chester, Montgomery, Shrewsbury, Bridgnorth, Leominster, Hereford, Monmouth, Chepstow and Ludlow quickly declared for the Royalist cause. Only Gloucester, a Puritan cloth-manufacturing centre, did not. Confident of good support from the west, the King went from Nottingham to Shrewsbury to raise troops from the area and from Wales.

The ordinary citizens who were unlucky enough to be seen by passing troops might have been expected to provide food or forage – with or without payment. While wealthier elements of society would have been expected to part with money for one or both sides of the conflict, for many though, there was little to disrupt everyday life.

However, within weeks of the start of the conflict the quiet little settlement of Bleathwood may have heard the clash of steel. Bleathwood was then, and is today, a quiet scattered community in the parish of Little Hereford in north Herefordshire, within a few miles of Tenbury.

Historical facts are few but it is possible that a significant skirmish took place here, for a map of the area dated 1754 has the symbol of a battle with the date 1642, and identifies a significant tree on the road from Burford to Ludlow called Standard Oak. Any oak present at the time has now disappeared but another small oak plantation and an intriguingly named coppice remain, which may indicate the site.

The skirmish, if it occurred, followed on from the first major military encounter of the war. Prince Rupert was the King's General of Horse, his nephew and a talented military tactician. He was 23 years old when, on Tuesday

20 September 1642, he left Bridgnorth with his men and rode to Worcester to cover Sir John Byron's withdrawal from the city carrying donations to the King's treasure. The treasure was in danger from advancing Parliamentarian troops under the overall command of the Earl of Essex.

The King's treasure travelled everywhere with him, for security reasons and also to pay for his and his troops' needs. As Worcester was in danger of falling to the Parliamentarian forces the treasure needed to be moved urgently to the King at Shrewsbury. Rupert remained behind to give the convoy time to get away safely.

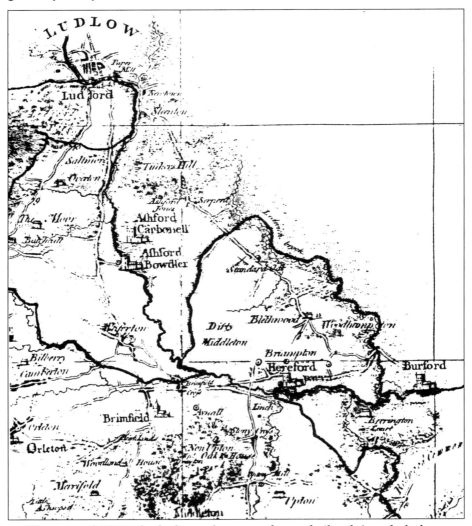

*The map of 1754 which shows the crossed swords 'battle' symbol above 'Standard Oak' at Bleathwood*

Rupert, with his troop of 500 horsemen and a number of dragoons, was waiting in Brickfield Meadow by Powick Bridge on Friday the 23rd, when an advance troop of 1,000 of Lord Essex's forces under the command of Nathaniel Fiennes was seen across the river.

A number of Parliamentarian horse charged across the bridge, led by Colonel Sandys, and were met by gunshot from Rupert's sentries and dragoons. Rupert marshalled his cavalry and led a counter charge. After 15 minutes 150 Parliamentarian troops were dead and Colonel Sandys was mortally wounded. Rupert suffered a sword injury, but the Parliamentarians were in rapid retreat. The outcome of the engagement served to enhance Prince Rupert's reputation.

Although Rupert may have then ridden to take over protection of the King's treasure, it is also likely that his presence was required with the King. The train containing the treasure and guards probably made slow progress up the Severn Valley, whilst Rupert turned to the Teme Valley to join the King at Shrewsbury via Tenbury and Ludlow.

According to a journal kept by one of Rupert's entourage, Rupert marched his troops through the night from Powick Bridge and arrived at Burford on Saturday 24 September, where he stayed overnight as a guest of the Baron of Burford. In all likelihood he needed to rest his injury as well as his men and horses. The following day he travelled on toward Ludlow, the most reasonable route being along the Bleathwood Road.

In the meantime, what of the Parliamentarian force? Their commander, the Earl of Essex, was an uninspired and gloomy man. His father had been a favourite of Queen Elizabeth I though she later had him beheaded for treason, and the son could be forgiven for having a cheerless childhood and subsequent gloomy outlook on life. One historian reports that Essex travelled with his coffin and shroud, considering them to be essential parts of a professional soldier's kit. He seems to have been argumentative and slow to make decisions and act on them, and it is unlikely that he ordered any pursuit of Rupert or his treasure.

However, a Colonel Hide may have been present in Essex's army. At one time Lieutenant Colonel to Colonel Sandys, Hide was a British mercenary with considerable experience in warfare from his time on the continent. It may be that he aimed to pursue Rupert.

What actually happened is subject to conjecture. The journal writer amongst Rupert's entourage refers to their arrival at Ludlow but also mentions 'a false alarm'. The symbol on the map is placed near several springs and where a small brook cuts across the Bleathwood Road between Halfway House and Burnt House Farm, very near the Herefordshire-Shropshire border. It is possible that Rupert had chosen to rest and water his horses at this spot. He may also have left a number of defensive troops behind or he may have had intelligence that led him to prepare an ambush.

Just how the fight unfolded, how large each of the opposing groups was, and how many died, if any, is entirely unknown. The fact that the skirmish at Bleathwood has no report in the history as recorded by the 'official London press', may mean that the battle did not go completely in favour of Parliament, who were in control of the capital. It is known that Ludlow suffered at the hands of a Parliamentary force a short time later, so they would have been trailing Rupert at least. The fact that the Royalists did not report this skirmish is not entirely surprising either. They were constantly on the move in various groups and had limited access to recording and printing in this part of the provinces. Such a localised and possibly small event may not have seemed notable enough to record and publish except in private diaries or letters. It may also be that the Royalists were under pressure of time or perhaps the outcome was not one that they wanted to record for posterity.

Bleathwood no doubt returned to its pastoral ways within a short time. However, it is not unlikely that immediately after the skirmish, residents were left to deal with any dead and dying. Yet no mention of burials of this time is made in Little Hereford, Burford, Ashford Carbonel or Ludlow parish records. However, a coppice near the brook still remains. It is called Deadnall Coppice. Is this where they lie?

# Flax Farming

Tenbury would not naturally be considered a site for a successful flax industry, but in the 18th century a great deal of it was in fact grown in the Teme Valley. (In the 16th century laws were passed enforcing its growth, the proportion being one rood of flax to every 60 acres. A rood is a quarter of an acre.)

Flax produced the most luxurious fibres known at the time but growing it required considerable commitment in terms of labour. Fine long flax fibres when spun and woven create linen, a hard-wearing fabric with a beautiful soft shine. The same plant also produced tougher fibres used for all manner of threads or fabrics, from sheets and smocks to sailcloth. Well made linen will last a century or more. In the 17th century, indicating its value, linen sold for 10d per yard, and a ready made shirt for 14s. At the same time, beef was 2d per pound and port wine 4s a gallon.

Evidence of the production of flax is found in field names that still exist in the Teme Valley, for example hemp and linacre. Flaxbed is found at Nash and Lineage is found on early maps of Castle Meadow around the Castle Tump on what is now the Shropshire side of the River Teme. The community of Lindridge may have derived its name from 'flax ridge'.

Since the process of turning flax fibre into yarn requires copious amounts of water, farms which grew flax were often located along river sides, hence the use of Castle Meadow. The plants could be retted (see the box overleaf) without running water or pools but required that water be brought to the fields, thus making it harder both to achieve and to control. However this process made for a whiter fibre. Too much soaking often made the fibres yellow.

*The church at Lindridge, a settlement which possibly took its name from the growing of flax*

Labour was required at all stages of the plant's growth from sowing to harvest. At harvest the plant had to be pulled from the ground rather than cut down. This was because the sought after fibres extended well into the roots. Once taken from the fields great amounts of time and skill were needed before the fibres were turned into fine linen thread.

In spite of the amount of time and energy required, flax seems to have been grown mainly for its fibre, although linseed oil is made from its seed. This yellowish oil is used for making paint, printers' ink, linoleum and in medicine as a laxative. In painting it is used either raw or boiled. Boiled oil absorbs oxygen from the air more quickly than the raw oil, so is preferable where paint is required to dry quickly. Linseed was also made into cattle cake, whilst the seeds could be pounded and mixed with boiling water to make a comforting 'linseed poultice' as a home remedy. The seeds, boiled, made a warm milky drink for feeding calves.

Flax, however, is a hungry plant and quickly exhausts the soil.

---

### Making Flax Plants into Fabric

RIPPLING: combing action to remove the seeds from the plant after it is pulled from the ground.

RETTING or ROTTING: soaking the sheaves of flax in water for several weeks to soften the hard outer fibres on the stem.

SCUTCHING: a beating action that breaks the hard outer fibres or shell off the stem.

HACKLING: a comb with very long nails through which the stems are drawn to remove any outer shell and also the shorter fibres that are known as tow.

DRESSING: separating and arranging the remaining long fibres in soft layers to tie to a distaff ready for spinning. The tow fibres are also spun and are used to make coarser fabrics.

DYEING: flax fibres may be dyed as yarn (line) or as the final fabric (linen). The material is first bleached by simmering in a bath of caustic soda and then laid out in the sun. It can then be dyed with vegetable dyes, although this is difficult unless a mordant or chemical is used to encourage the adhesion of the dye. Mordants are made from iron (an iron pot), oak apples, bark or twigs.

WEAVING: a common fabric was made by weaving bleached and unbleached yarn in patterns. The unbleached yarn was stabilised from fading in sunlight by soaking it in a strong solution of juniper juice and water.

FABRIC BLEACHING: In the medieval household linen fabric was 'bucked'. The linen was packed in deep barrels, with bent sticks between the folds, and a strong lye, variously made of wood ash, urine and rainwater, was poured in from the top. After repeated soakings the linen was taken out, beaten and repacked, then fresh water run through. This process was called 'leying bucks' or passing the ley through the buck. The linen was then spread out to dry and bleach in the sun.

# Women in Local History

It would seem that women have been almost invisible in recorded history. But a closer look at the records shows that they had a significant part in daily, legal, business and economic life and in many cases wielded considerable power.

Housewifery has always had little positive press, but it was the power that drove many a family enterprise. Alongside it went labouring in the family business and where that was agriculture, working in the fields alongside men. Women who acted as manager of the home were therefore also specialists in everything from veterinary needs to midwifery, and from food preservation to pest control. Their roles from earliest times to present history were anything but subservient. But the records of these everyday enterprises are scarce.

In Anglo-Saxon and Norman nobility, where the earliest historical evidence survives, women were able to inherit land, hold, use and later dispose of it as they wished. Widows had special provision and customarily were entitled to one third of the husband's estate, although it may have been as much as half, two thirds, or even all of it. If, however, she remarried within a year, these lands reverted to the husband's kin. Other assets, such as jewellery and housing, remained the wife's and reverted to her kin on her death. These customs survived in various forms well into the 17th century.

Women did not take their husband's name as a matter of course and there were no fixed rules about this. The convention gradually filtered down from the landowning classes where surnames were part of the hereditary process. Some surnames were feminine forms of male occupations such as Webster (weaver), Baxter (baker), Brewster (brewer), Dexter (dyer), indicating that women clearly had command of many parts of business life either in their own rights or as partners of their husbands.

In the middle ages, marriage contracts often went into great detail, outlining what the wife (if her family were well enough off) would contribute to the marriage, usually in the form of land, but also prescribing what she would receive if widowed and what provisions would be made for her children. Thus:

Indenture tripartite made the fourth and twentieth day of May 1649, between Sir Gilbert Cornewall, Knight and Baron of Burford and Dame Elizabeth his wife and Thomas Cornewall Esq the eldest son and heir of the first part and Sir Thomas Reade of Dunstew in the county of Oxford knight of the second part and others of the third part …

… in consideration of a marriage to be shortly solemnized between the said Thomas Cornewall and Dame Anne Read eldest daughter of Thomas Read … if this marriage take effect and she happen to survive and outlive the said Thomas Cornewall her intended husband … some of the lands and hereditament of Sir Gilbert Cornewall … during their natural lives and the life of the longest liver of them without impeachment … in full recompense of her Dower … provisions for their lawful sons … several sums of money for the daughters of Thomas and Anne for their marriage portions …

Lease agreements were often made in the name of both husband and wife and the term 'three lives' on a copyhold agreement often involved both of them along with a son or grandson. The object of 'three lives' was to make the tenancy for as long a period as possible, for during that time the rent would be fixed – only to be re-negotiated at the end of the term. If the wife was party to the agreement she could not be removed from the land or business even on the death of her husband.

Agreements in sale or purchase also involved women, thereby making it evident that they were seen to be equal partners in the ownership of land or property, as in the following indenture of 1679 regarding land.

This indenture made 10 August 1679 between Susan Rowbery of Tenbury and William Cupper of Tenbury of one part and Richard Tomlins of Tenbury and Elizabeth his wife: Susan Rowberry and William Cupper pay to Richard Tomlins the sum of nine pounds for three parcels of arable land containing about two acres, one acre, and a half acre.

Other examples show women independently powerful. In 1777 a Deed of Sale was made between Anne Pardoe (spinster) and the delightfully named Dansey Dansey, the lord of the Little Hereford manor. Under the terms of the agreement, Miss Pardoe paid £1,000 '… for lands in township of Middleton, Parish of Little Hereford …'. Mr Dansey had the right to buy back the land at £1,000 plus 4% per annum '… at 14 day October next …'. One can suspect that this was a short-term loan with security of land involving a substantial amount of money!

Many women were executors of their husbands' estates and guardians of the children and continued to run their husbands' business after their deaths.

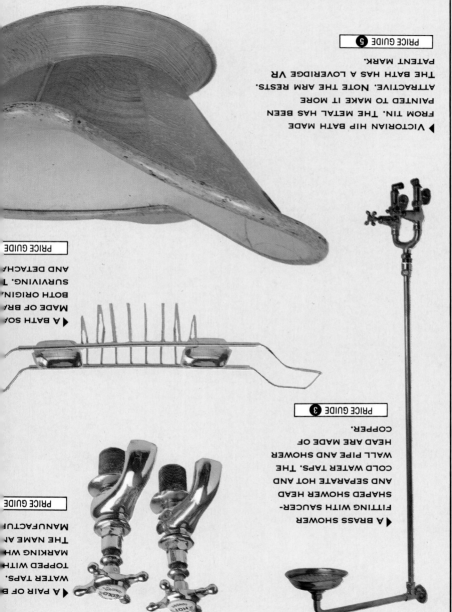

the 1880s and 90s had often become domestic works of art. The great makers included Shanks, Twyfords and Doulton, who also introduced the bathroom suite, in which loo,

floral swags and stripes, and pictorial hunting scenes.

Feet were either in cast iron or brass and designed in the ball-and-claw or paw style. Sometimes there was foliage

than the m... Hand-show... particularly free-standin... standing up... what precar...

**PRICE GUIDE 5**

◀ VICTORIAN HIP BATH MADE FROM TIN. THE METAL HAS BEEN PAINTED TO MAKE IT MORE ATTRACTIVE. NOTE THE ARM RESTS. THE BATH HAS A LOVERIDGE VR PATENT MARK.

**PRICE GUIDE 3**

◀ A BRASS SHOWER FITTING WITH SAUCER-SHAPED SHOWER HEAD AND SEPARATE HOT AND COLD WATER TAPS. THE WALL PIPE AND SHOWER HEAD ARE MADE OF COPPER.

**PRICE GUIDE**

◀ A BATH SO... MADE OF BR... BOTH ORIGIN... SURVIVING, T... AND DETACH...

**PRICE GUIDE**

◀ A PAIR OF B... WATER TAPS, TOPPED WITH MARKING WH... THE NAME AN... MANUFACTUR...

· PRICE GUIDE ·

For example, the Will of Edward Bowen, a hop merchant of Tenbury, in 1683 left everything to his wife with the exception of a few bequests of £5 to brothers, sisters and other relatives and to Elizabeth Lane, 'daughter of my brother-in-law William Lane the sum of twenty pounds and one feather bed to be paid her when she cometh to the age of one and twenty years'. His wife was made 'sole executrix of this my last will and testament and to pay the several legacies within one year after the date herself in witness here of I have here unto put my hand and seal the day and year first above written'.

The Will of William Holloway of Tenbury, yeoman, was made on 28 January 1852 (he died in April 1853) and he left several messuages in Trumpet Yard and five cottages in Church Street to his two daughters, Elizabeth Holloway and Frances Palmer. To Elizabeth Holloway he also left a dwelling house in Teme Street (next to Lloyds Bank), and the house next

*This is the last Will and Testament of me Sarah Foster of Tenbury in the County of Worcester Spinster I devise and bequeath all my real and personal property of every description unto my Nephew James Bishop and my Niece Matilda Bishop (Children of my late Sister Penelope Bishop) Upon trust to sell and convert the same into money and to stand possessed of the nett proceeds after payment of my debts funeral and testamentary expenses Upon trust for them the said James Bishop and Matilda Bishop and their Sister my Niece Fanny the Wife of Thomas Price to be equally divided between them as tenants in common And if either of them the said James Bishop Matilda Bishop or Fanny Price shall happen to die in my lifetime leaving a child or children who shall survive me then I direct that such child or children shall take (if children as tenants in common) the share of my estate which his her or their parent would have taken had he or she survived me I appoint the said James Bishop and Matilda Bishop to be Executor and Executrix of this my Will And I revoke all previous Wills Witness my hand this fifteenth day of May One thousand eight hundred and and eighty five —— The Mark of X Sarah Foster —— Signed by the said Sarah Foster the Testatrix as and for her last Will and Testament in the presence of us (both present at the same time) who in her presence at her request and in the presence of each other have hereunto subscribed our names as attesting Witnesses the above Will having first been read over to the Testatrix in our presence when she appeared perfectly to understand the same —— Wm S Davis, Solr Tenbury ——*

*The last 'Will and Testament of Sarah Foster of Tenbury made in 1885*

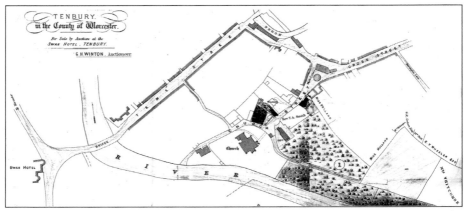

*A plan of 'several valuable freehold landed investments' that accompanied details of a sale to be held in May 1879 at the Swan Hotel, Tenbury. Miss Holland, Mrs Withington, Mrs Nott and Mrs Whitcombe are noted amongst the neighbouring landowners*

door to his granddaughter, Frances Holloway. To his son, Thomas Holloway, he left the West Field.

Most married women did not make wills as their property was considered to belong to their husband. However many widows and spinsters or those with independent ownership did. Thus probate was granted on the Will of Elizabeth Critott of Sutton, Worcester, made on 26 October 1765, 'whereby she gave and devised to Edward Downes the houses and land in Tenbury for his lifetime …'. The Will of Elizabeth Holloway mentioned above, made on 21 November 1859, bequeathed the dwelling house in Teme Street that she had inherited just six years before to her two sisters, Mary Reynolds and Frances Palmer, along with her share in the houses in Trumpet Yard.

It may be assumed that women had few rights and this would be true in so much as their affairs were largely in the control of men. But it must not be assumed that they were powerless or thrown on the charity of family or church if left alone. Many were powerful enough to command legal respect, be looked after even in their widowhood and influence small and large affairs in hundreds of individual ways.

# Law and Order in Tenbury

It is hard to imagine anywhere as peaceful as Tenbury. However it has had its moments of high drama, farcical comedy and mundane lawlessness.

A police force as we know it did not exist in England until the 19th century. Until that time, local matters were dealt with by church courts, the local watchman, manorial courts or the town elders. Major matters such as riot or insurrection were put in the hands of the military, but Tenbury seems to have escaped the need for these latter services.

After the Civil War (1642-1646) systems of law, order and punishment were improved with fairer trial systems and more reasonable punishment, although hanging for the smallest crimes meant that law was upheld by fear, and the flogging of men and women still took place. There is reference to the town stocks and whipping post in Tenbury well into recent history. Prisons were farmed out to a gaoler who made his profit from the prisoners.

In 1772 an association for the prosecution of felons was formed at Tenbury, as was the case in many Worcestershire villages. Poaching and stealing of farm produce and livestock was rife, and under an Act of 1770 people convicted of such crimes could now be imprisoned and for a second offence publicly whipped.

The following case of a family falling out was reported in the local paper on Tuesday 25 May 1775:

> ... on Friday morning last the following dire catastrophe happened at Thomas Stinton's shoemaker, at Boraston ...
>
> His mother, about 70 years of age, from an avaritious [sic] disposition, and an unnatural disaffection towards her son, his wife and children, with whom she lived attempted to destroy them by conveying a quantity of arsenic into the teapot amongst the tea from which they were to breakfast. The youngest child (an infant of 15 months old) being in a state of dentition; it was thought necessary by the mother to give it a dose of rhubarb, which was to have been administered, in a cup of tea that morning, but the child happily discovered an unusual nauseous taste, refused the medicine, though the old woman inhumanly endeavoured to

25

oblige the infant to take it, and being thus prejudiced, the child refused likewise to drink of the tea prepared for breakfast. The mother, however with one of her children, drank it, and found a disagreeable taste, but attributed it to the sugar; the father offered his tea to the old woman, who refused it. In a short time the mother and child who had breakfasted; were seized with a violent sickness; vomiting and a pain in the stomach, which continuing several hours. Mr Cheese of Tenbury was sent for by whose skill and assiduity the poison was expelled and they were happily preserved. During this interval, the old woman had attempted to wash the teapot in a tub of water, but was prevented. This, together with her refusal to breakfast of the tea, occasioned strong suspicions of her perpetrating the diabolical act, which being related to Mr Cheese, who observing the symptoms in the old woman exactly corresponding with those of mother and daughter, immediately directed her to be searched whereupon a cord and an old knife were found in her pocket and a large paper of arsenic in her bosom. She obdurately refused every means of recovery and expired in great agonies the same evening, without making any confession than that of taking a large quantity of arsenic dry, and afterwards drinking cold water.

The Coroner's Inquest sat the next day and brought in the verdict 'Felo de fe' [suicide].

In 1821 William Mantle of Tenbury was executed at the County Gaol for stealing sheep. It was reported that 'The ropes were newly extended to their length when tied around culprit's neck, so that scarcely any fall took place. He died in great agony.'

In 1822 Robert Peel took over the Home Office and immediately brought in reform of criminal law. He abolished the death penalty for a great number of crimes and in 1829 established the first civilian police force, often called Bobbies or Peelers to this day. Although set up in London first of all, in the course of a generation, forces were adopted all over the country.

One of the first policemen in Tenbury was George Checketts, who began his service in 1840. He was a member of the Worcester Constabulary for 48 years and was in the force until he was past 70. He died in 1906. In his early years the Police Station at Tenbury was a kind of shed, but it was insecure so prisoners were taken to The Ship public house and handcuffed to an iron bar that had been fixed in one of the rooms for the purpose.

John Haynes, another well known Tenbury police sergeant, was born in Churchill near Chipping Norton, Oxfordshire in 1845. He joined the Worcestershire Constabulary as a 4th Class Constable on 1 June 1866. According to his records he was 22 years old when he joined, 5 feet 8 inches tall and weighed 11 stone. He was paid 4s 10d a week, about twice that of an average farm labourer. He married Alice Lucas on 21 January 1868 and they had 14 children, three of whom died in infancy. He served as Sergeant at Tenbury from February 1885 until 31 March 1894 when he retired. Sergeant Long (who probably preceded Sergeant Haynes at Tenbury) was promoted to Divisional Sergeant of Police at Redditch in February 1885.

Sergeant Haynes often appeared in newspaper reports. The *Tenbury Wells Advertiser* of 14 April 1885 carries news of a case brought before the Worcestershire Easter Quarter Sessions. Felix Faulkner, a labourer aged 62, was charged with stealing 17s 6d from William Finch. Faulkner had left the house where he lodged with Finch, and was pursued by DS Haynes who asked him for the money. Faulkner denied he had it, but DS Haynes searched him and found 17s 1d concealed in the lining of his trousers. The coins were the same that Finch had lost. In court, Faulkner was convicted by a jury and sentenced to three months hard labour.

*John Haynes with two of his children*

On 12 March 1889, Haynes received information that Maria Corke, a servant girl whose father lived at Highwood, was wanted on a charge of stealing a lady's half hoop gold ring worth £50 from her employer in St Johns Wood, London. Sergeant Haynes duly apprehended her at Highwood and informed the Metropolitan Police. She was remanded in custody.

The cases with which he had to deal were quite varied, as the following report in the *Tenbury Wells Advertiser* for 14 April 14 1891 shows:

> Gilbert Bayliss, Little Red Wood Farm was charged with stealing eight fowls, property of James Froggatt, Old Wood Farm. ... Sergeant Haynes stated: on Monday the 6th, I went to Mr Froggatt's farm at Old Wood; I saw prints of a man's foot about eight yards from the Wainhouse, each way to Herefordshire to a distance of about 70 yards from the prisoner's house, which is about a mile from Old Wood Farm; I afterwards went with Mr Froggatt to Ludlow market, and saw the two fowls which I

# WORCESTERSHIRE CONSTABULARY.

## DESCRIPTIVE REGISTER AND RECORD OF SERVICE OF

### John Haynes.

| | |
|---|---|
| Date of Appointment as Constable ... | 1st June 1866. |
| Warrant Number ... ... ... | 945 |
| Divisional Number ... ... ... | 115 |
| Age ... ... ... ... ... | 22 |
| Height ... ... ... ... ... | 5ft 8 |
| Weight ... ... ... ... ... | 11 Stone |
| Chest Measurement ... ... ... | 3 9 inches |
| Head Measure for Helmet ... ... | 6 7/8 |
| Complexion ... ... ... ... | Fresh |
| Eyes ... ... ... ... ... | Grey. |
| Hair ... ... ... ... ... | Brown |
| Particular Marks ... ... ... | |
| Where Born — in the Parish of ... ... | Churchill |
| — in or near the Town of ... | Chipping Norton |
| — in the County of ... ... | Oxford. |
| Religious Persuasion ... ... ... | Church of England |
| Trade or Calling ... ... ... | Laborer |
| Education ... ... ... ... | |
| Last Place of Residence ... ... ... | Churchill |
| What Public Service ... ... ... | Nil |
| Regiment, Corps, Police, &c. ... ... | |
| Length of Service ... ... ... | |
| Amount of Pension ... ... ... | |
| When Discharged ... ... ... | |
| If in Army Reserve ... ... ... | |
| With whom last Employed ... ... | A. Andrews Esq |
| Where last Employed ... ... ... | Saroden, nr Chipping Norton |
| If Vaccinated ... ... ... ... | Yes |
| If in any Sick Club or Benefit Society ... | Foresters |
| Weekly Amount when Sick ... ... | 12/- |
| Single or Married ... ... ... | Married |
| Maiden Name of Wife, and Date of Marriage | Alice Lucas. 21st January 1868. |
| Native Place of Wife ... ... ... | Lea Marston, Warwickshire. |
| Number of Children and Dates of Birth | William 1840. John 1842. Elizabeth 1874. Richard 1876. Nellie 1879. Walter 1880. Alfred Walter 1883. Ernest 1884. Frank 1885. Beatrice 1887. Maud. 1888. |

I hereby declare that the above particulars relating to me are to the best of my belief fully and truly stated.

Signed John Haynes

now produce taken from two crates belonging to Mr Baker, which Mr Froggatt identified as his property; I took possession of them and shortly afterwards the prisoner in Ludlow, and charged him with stealing eight or nine fowls, the property of Mr Froggatt and selling them in the market; he replied 'I sold none but my own;' in his coat pocket I found a quantity of feathers, which I produce – The Justices, after a short consultation, said they had found him guilty of the offence, but they would not send him to prison being his first offence, but would fine him £2 and £1 2s costs, in default of payment 14 days hard labour.

However, at times Haynes could perhaps be somewhat overzealous, as this case in the *Tenbury Wells Advertiser* on 15 September 1891 indicates:

William Postans, horse-breaker, Knighton-on-Teme, was summoned by DS Haynes for being drunk in charge of a horse on 3rd of August last. From the evidence of Supt. Pugh, and Sergt. Haynes, it appeared that defendant had been at the Foresters' fete. About 8:30 p.m. he was

Name *John Haynes.*

| Promotions, Reductions, &c. | Rate of Pay per Day | | PERIODS. | | Years. | Days |
|---|---|---|---|---|---|---|
| | | | From | To | | |
| Appointed as 4th Class Constable | 2 | 6 | 1st June 66 | 30 June 66 | | 30 |
| 3rd Class Constable | 2 | 10 | 1st July 1866 | 30 April 1868 | 1 | 30? |
| 2nd " " | 3 | . | 1st May 68 | 14 July 72 | 4 | 76 |
| 1st " " | 3 | 2 | 15 July 1872 | 14 July 73 | 1 | . |
| 1st " " | 3 | 4 | 15 July 1873 | 14 July 74 | 4 | . |
| " " " | 3 | 6 | 15 July 1874 | 14 Nov 78 | 1 | 122 |
| Sergeant. | 4 | . | 15 Nov 1878 | 14 Nov 83 | 5 | . |
| " " | 4 | 3 | 15 Nov 1883 | 14 Nov 88 | 5 | . |
| " " | 4 | 6 | 15 Nov 1888 | 31 March 92 | 3 | 13? |
| " " | 5 | . | 1st April 1892 | 31st March 94 | 2 | . |
| | | | | | 27 | 304 |

| STATIONS TO WHICH APPOINTED AND DURATION OF SERVICE IN EACH. | | | | |
|---|---|---|---|---|
| Name of Station. | From | To | Years. | Days |
| 1. Head Quarters. | 1st June 1866 | 11th July 1866 | | 41 |
| 2. Great Witley | 12th July 1866 | 12 May 68 | 1 | 30 |
| 3. Astley. | 13 May 1868 | 27 June 69 | 1 | 4 |
| 4. Broadwaters | 28 June 1869 | 28 Feby 72 | 2 | 24 |
| 5. Fernhill Heath | 1st March 1872 | 24 Nov 78 | 6 | 27 |
| 6. Suckley | 25 Nov 1878 | 8 Feby 85 | 6 | 7 |
| 7. Tenbury | 9 Feby 1885 | 31st March 94 | 9 | 5 |
| | | | 27 | 304 |

*This page and opposite: John Haynes' Register and Record of Service with Worcestershire Constabulary*

riding a colt down the street. Seeing that he was drunk, DS Haynes went to him and told him that he had better let the horse stop at the Oak and go home alone. The defendant wanted the policeman to take him to a doctor, who should examine him as to whether he was drunk or not. The policeman said, 'Go to a doctor yourself if you want to.' PCs Brazier and Davies then came up and took the horse and put it in the stable adjoining the police station. Samuel Gore said in his opinion the defendant was capable of taking care of the horse, but he did not think he was sober. In defence Postans called John Bond, King's Head; John Hewitt, builder; Hugh Grandfield, farmer; Alfred Walker, hay dealer; and William Howells, builder, who said the defendant appeared to be perfectly sober, but very much excited on one of the men threatening to pull him off the horse. The magistrates were of the opinion that there was some doubt in the case, and dismissed it.

Sometime before 1891 Sergeant Haynes had been joined in Tenbury by PC Davies and the two men were involved in a hot pursuit recorded in the *Tenbury Wells Advertiser* for 21 July 1891:

William Hurds (14), Harry Hurds (13), Ernest Grice (13) and Moses Round (13) were charged with stealing ten bottles of perry of the value of 10s 8d, on the 28th June, the property of Arthur Walker, cider merchant, Tenbury. Arthur Walker stated: On Sunday, June 28, about 8:30 p.m. I went down to my cider premises and found three boys there William Hurds, Harry Hurds and Ernest Grice. As soon as I saw them I shouted to them; they were in a small nursery in my orchard; they jumped the fence and ran down the Burgage Meadow; I ran after them; they went over the Kyre brook; I turned back again and came to the police-station, where I obtained the assistance of Sergt. Haynes and PC Davies and we all went in pursuit of the boys; PC Davies and I went down the Rise lane; when we got opposite the railings at the entrance to the Palmers ashbed; PC Davies jumped over the palings and the boys commenced to run and he followed them up the hill; I turned back and found William Hurds in the custody of DS Haynes; I asked the boy what brought him on my cider premises and trespassing by Mr Smith's grass and he said 'I didn't have any of it.' I remarked that he would hear further of it. Sergt Haynes and I went down to the cider stores and examined the premises; we found near where the boys had been stood five bottles of perry and I knew then that the premises had been broken into; we unlocked the wooden warehouse, and found a case broken open and sixteen bottles taken out …

On occasion the police were not supported by the population and perhaps managed to even exacerbate a situation:

Enoch Morgan of Tenbury who had been liberated out on bail was charged by PC Davies with having been drunk and disorderly in Cross street, Tenbury on Saturday night, February 3rd. He was further charged with assaulting that officer in the execution of his duty at the same time. Defendant pleaded not guilty to both offences. PC Davies stated that about 10 p.m. on the night in question he saw defendant at the Cross street end of Berrington road in a drunken condition and heard him using filthy language. He requested him to go home and be quiet, but he refused, and witness told him that if he did not do so he should lock him up. As soon as he went to lay hold of him, he struck him a blow on the chest. He then brought defendant as far as Market square, where he had to get the assistance of Sergt Haynes to take him to the station, as he behaved like a madman. A crowd of roughs were behind them trying to get defendant away, and about 150 people were present ... Sergt Haynes said he met PC Davies bringing defendant down Cross street, and he told him to take defendant to the station. A number of people were about. Witness afterwards saw defendant struggling with PC Davies in Market square and in consequence assisted in taking him to the station. A crowd got round them and tried to get defendant away.

George Bufton said he was at the end of Berrington road when PC Davies came up and struck a cripple on the leg with a stick. He requested them to move on and some did ... Davies then went into the crowd and said, 'I'll show you whether I can summon you for staying here,' and he then made a rush at defendant and pushed him down. Defendant got up and said to Davies, 'You have been waiting for this some time.' Davies then took out a book and began to write in it.

The Chairman stated that the Bench had no doubt defendant was drunk, but not disorderly and they should dismiss both cases.

In another incident, the *Tenbury Wells Advertiser* for 22 January 1889 notes that George Morris of Burford charged DS Haynes with assaulting him. He alleged he was standing in Market Square when Haynes came up and ordered him off the pavement. He declined to do so, and said that Haynes then pushed him off. In this instance the case was dismissed with the Chairman of the Bench saying 'The public ought to support the police.'

Not all the cases mentioned in the papers included drunkenness or rowdy behaviour. For example the *Tenbury Wells Advertiser* for Tuesday 21 July 1891 includes the following variety:

Tenbury Petty Session: Tuesday.
Before the Rev. E.G. Baldwyn Childe, G. Wallace, Esq., and Rev. T. Bengough.

The Food and Drugs Act: John Barnes, grocer of Tenbury was summoned for selling mustard adulterated with 15 pints of farina, on the

29th May last to PC John Holloway. Defendant stated that the mustard was supplied by Messrs Keen and he was under the impression that it was pure. Fined £2 plus costs.

George Smallman, of the Talbot Hotel, Newham Bridge was charged with selling gin adulterated with 40 percent of water, the law allowing 35 per cent, to PC John Holloway. Defendant admitted that the analysis was correct, but explained that the gin was kept in the cellar for some time and probably its strength had decreased by evaporation or some other cause. ... The Chairman said that he would accept, in part, this explanation, but the Justices felt they must convict, and fined him ...

Before Rev. E.G. Baldwyne Childe, G. Wallace, Esq and E.V.V. Wheeler, Esq.

Allowing a Nuisance to Exist: Isabella Bridgewater, Thomas Price, James Golley and Albert Austis of Cross-street were summoned by Mr H. Wall, Sanitary Inspector for allowing a nuisance to exist on their premises. ... notice and been served on the defendants to empty an offensive cesspit, which was in a state injurious to health. ... defendants were neighbours and there was a disagreement amongst them as to whose place it was to have the cesspit cleared, the four closets emptying into each other. The defendants were fined 5s each and the costs, and the nuisance must be abated within three days.

John Haynes ended his career at Tenbury on 31 March 1894 having spent 27 years in the force. His retirement pension was £60 16s 8d per year. After retirement he became the landlord of the Collier's Arms at Rock, but remained in the news, as this item in the papers for 12 June 1894 notes:

Mr J. Haynes, late sergeant of police at Tenbury and now landlord of the Colliers' Arms Inn, at Rock, near Bewdley, writes to complain of a report by some evil-disposed person or persons, circulated in Tenbury that he had been fined for being drunk on his licensed premises. There is no truth in the report, and as such rumours are calculated to damage his character and annoy him, he offers £2 reward to any person who will give him information which shall prove who originated the scandal.

Later John Haynes became landlord of the Dog Inn in Dunley. He died in 1901 at the age of 57.

There can be little doubt that, in general, Tenbury was grateful for the support it received from its generations of policemen. How nice it is to see them back.

# The Baptist Schools and Public Education

In the early 19th century, education for poor children was a haphazard affair. There were some small 'dame' schools – schools set up by single women (and sometimes men) in their living rooms – which were not much more than child minding establishments. Other schools were run by charities but there was no organized system for the poor. The rural poor were particularly neglected although not ignored entirely.

In 1811 the Church of England formed The National Society for Promoting the Education of the Poor in the Principles of the Established Church. The British and Foreign School Society was also establishing schools in Hereford and adjoining areas; while shortly after, the trustees of Edward Goff's estate were founding free schools for the poor.

Edward Goff was an interesting individual. Self-made and almost illiterate, he was born in Huntington, near Kington, Herefordshire, in 1738. His family was poor, and with no education he went to London and started in the coal business – at the very bottom as a coal heaver. He managed to educate himself, eventually becoming a wealthy coal merchant with premises in Scotland Yard. He was also a deeply religious man, a Calvinist, and when he retired from business, he was determined to give some poor children the education he had missed.

When he died in 1813 he left a large sum specifically to found schools in and around Herefordshire. One of them was created in Tenbury.

Although not a Baptist himself, Goff had great respect for them and included them as trustees of his estate. His schools, however, were for all children free of charge. Thirty-two Goff Schools were established and four of them still exist in Hay-on-Wye, Gorsley, Longhope (near Ross-on-Wye) and Eastcombe (near Stroud).

In 1816, the Baptists began a Goff's School in Tenbury. This caused considerable alarm among the local people who feared that children attending the school would be indoctrinated in the Baptist faith. The situation was described in dramatic terms in the minutes of the Baptist Chapel:

The principle [*sic*] inhabitants of the town were filled with consternation and dread saying the church will be overthrown if we do not do something

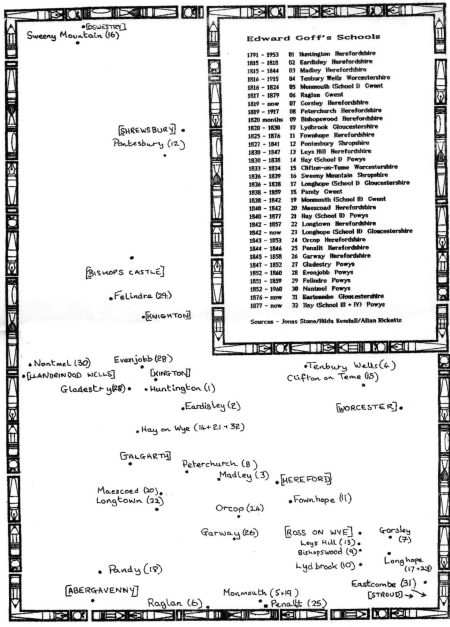

**Edward Goff's Schools**

| | | |
|---|---|---|
| 1791 – 1953 | 01 | Huntington Herefordshire |
| 1815 – 1818 | 02 | Eardisley Herefordshire |
| 1815 – 1844 | 03 | Madley Herefordshire |
| 1816 – 1915 | 04 | Tenbury Wells Worcestershire |
| 1816 – 1824 | 05 | Monmouth (School I) Gwent |
| 1817 – 1879 | 06 | Raglan Gwent |
| 1819 – now | 07 | Gorsley Herefordshire |
| 1819 – 1917 | 08 | Peterchurch Herefordshire |
| 1820 months | 09 | Bishopswood Herefordshire |
| 1820 – 1830 | 10 | Lydbrook Gloucestershire |
| 1825 – 1876 | 11 | Fownhope Herefordshire |
| 1827 – 1841 | 12 | Pontesbury Shropshire |
| 1830 – 1847 | 13 | Leys Hill Herefordshire |
| 1830 – 1838 | 14 | Hay (School I) Powys |
| 1833 – 1834 | 15 | Clifton-on-Teme Worcestershire |
| 1836 – 1839 | 16 | Sweeny Mountain Shropshire |
| 1836 – 1838 | 17 | Longhope (School I) Gloucestershire |
| 1838 – 1859 | 18 | Pandy Gwent |
| 1838 – 1842 | 19 | Monmouth (School II) Gwent |
| 1840 – 1842 | 20 | Maescoad Herefordshire |
| 1840 – 1877 | 21 | Hay (School II) Powys |
| 1842 – 1857 | 22 | Longtown Herefordshire |
| 1842 – now | 23 | Longhope (School II) Gloucestershire |
| 1843 – 1853 | 24 | Orcop Herefordshire |
| 1844 – 1846 | 25 | Penallt Herefordshire |
| 1845 – 1858 | 26 | Garway Herefordshire |
| 1847 – 1852 | 27 | Gladestry Powys |
| 1852 – 1860 | 28 | Evenjobb Powys |
| 1851 – 1859 | 29 | Felindre Powys |
| 1852 – 1960 | 30 | Nantmel Powys |
| 1876 – now | 31 | Eastcombe Gloucestershire |
| 1877 – now | 32 | Hay (School III + IV) Powys |

Sources – Jonas Stone/Hilda Kendall/Allan Ricketts

Map labels: [OSWESTRY], Sweeny Mountain (16), [SHREWSBURY], Pontesbury (12), [BISHOPS CASTLE], Felindre (29), [KNIGHTON], Nantmel (30), Evenjobb (28), [LLANDRINDOD WELLS], [KINGTON], Tenbury Wells (4), Clifton on Teme (15), Gladestry (28), Huntington (1), Eardisley (2), [WORCESTER], Hay on Wye (14+21+32), [TALGARTH], Peterchurch (8), Madley (3), [HEREFORD], Maescoed (20), Longtown (22), Orcop (24), Fownhope (11), Garway (26), [ROSS ON WYE], Gorsley (7), Leys Hill (13), Bishopswood (9), Longhope (17+23), Pandy (18), Lydbrook (10), Eastcombe (31), [ABERGAVENNY], Monmouth (5+19), [STROUD] →, Raglan (6), Penallt (25)

*A drawing showing the distribution of Goff schools and major towns in Herefordshire and adjoining counties*

to stop the progress of these invaders – how great a matter a little fire kindleth – and of the multitude of vain measures they adopted to stay the hand of omnipotence. I'll mention two or three. First it was proposed that certain Acts established in the reign of Charles the Second which had long been cast aside as being too absurd and tyrannical should be called to their aid. Consequently they had these obsolete laws printed as handbills and put them as it were in fresh force, threatening fines and imprisonment to those who preached or heard [the Baptist Doctrine].

Through the kind interference of our friends in Worcester other handbills appeared stating the present laws for the defence and protection of dissenters and the punishment to be inflicted on those who in any way molested them. The latter handbills soon cleared the former out of sight even as the morning light dissipates gloomy darkness.

Another resolution was made by the staunch supporters of their Mother Church, viz, they should combine in taking employment from those who attended this new place of worship and in this way 'crush the wretches'. Little, ah, little did they think of that superior and superintending power that made the rage and fury of His enemies and says 'hitherto shalt thou go but no further'.

Again another plan was adopted. The lovers of Darkness rather than Light imagined the [new Baptist] school accelerated the Process of Dissent and was one of the most effectual means to accomplish the overthrow of the Church. They exclaimed, 'the children will all be made Methodists [sic]' and to undermine this stratagem they summoned forth their powers by subscription to establish an opposition school, which was pursued with the utmost ardour. Thus were the strongrooms of wrath (which had long been sealed up from charity) opened and rendered that quite easy which for years before had been utterly impossible.

At a meeting on 16 May 1816 a Board of Trustees was set up to establish the new 'opposition school' as the Baptists described it. This was a National School under the aegis of the Church of England's National Society, known as the Tenbury National Madras School. It was founded by voluntary subscriptions, legacies and payments by those parents who could afford it. Premises were hired from Thomas Brookholding Jones for £20 per annum. It is not known where this was but three rooms in the building, probably in Cross Street, were adapted to form one large schoolroom by Mr Mills, a mason, who was assisted by Thomas Middleton, wheelwright; Samuel Crane, glazier; George Dukes, blacksmith; and Messrs Smith, joiners, at a cost of £108 7s. The school opened on 1 July 1816.

The children's ages ranged from 6 to 14. The Reverend J. Miller provided books, slates, quill pens, pencils and paper at a cost of £15 15s 4d, and Mr Grey of Bockleton School was engaged to organise the new school at a cost of £3 19s 6d. The first Master, Mr Benjamin Home, had been sent to the National

Society's Central School in London to learn how to operate the Madras or monitorial system of teaching. His expenses are shown in the document reproduced opposite and summarised here:

**Tenbury National Madras School**
**Subtreasurer's Account**

| Receipts | £ | s | d |
|---|---|---|---|
| Donations | 141 | 3 | 0 |
| Subscriptions in advance | 7 | 2 | 0 |
| Collection at the Church | 33 | 3 | 0 |
| Total Receipts | 181 | 8 | 0 |
| Total Disbursements | 136 | 17 | 7 |
| Balance in Subtreasurer's hand – 1st Septr 1816 | 44 | 10 | 5 |

| State of the Fund | £ | s | d |
|---|---|---|---|
| Balance in hand | 44 | 10 | 5 |
| Donations not yet received | 2 | 16 | 6 |
| Total | 47 | 6 | 11 |

Bills &c to be paid:
- Eaton for Slates — 5. 2. 11
- Society for books — 5. 15. 2
- Half a year's Salary to the Master at Xmas — 25. 0. 0
- Half a year's rent at £8 after deduct 16/ the charge for repairing the Steps — 9. 4. 0
- 45. 2. 1
- ... towards the Stove — 2. 4. 10

**Disbursements**

Bills for repairing & altering School Room

| | £ | s | d |
|---|---|---|---|
| Edwd Mills Mason first Bill | 34 | 17 | 0 |
| Do 2nd Bill | 0 | 6 | 0 |
| Thos Middleton Wheelwright 1st Bill | 38 | 2 | 6 |
| Do 2nd Bill | 2 | 8 | 6 |
| Saml Crane Glazier 1st Bill | 15 | 17 | 0 |
| Do 2nd Bill | 0 | 12 | 6 |
| Geo Jukes Blacksmith 1st Bill | 2 | 12 | 0 |
| Do 2nd Bill | 2 | 2 | 0 |
| Thos Evans Brazier Bill for Ventilators &c | | | |
| Messrs Smith Joiners Bill (including Church Benches) | | | |
| Total Bills for repairs £ | | | |

**Incidentals**

| | £ | s | d |
|---|---|---|---|
| Mr B Flome's Coachhire &c to & from the National School to qualify as Master of this | 11 | 7 | 0 |
| Do a Bill for printing | 7 | 16 | 0 |
| Compliment to Mr Gray for organising the School | 2 | 2 | 0 |
| Bill at the King's Head for his board & lodging | 1 | 17 | 6 |
| Jas Merrick Bill for Sand &c | 0 | 12 | 0 |
| A Ream of fools-cap paper | 1 | 3 | 0 |
| Carr: of box of Slates & waggon | 1 | 0 | 5 |
| Carr: of books & coach | 0 | 13 | 8 |
| School clock, case & fixing same | 1 | 15 | 6 |
| Posts to & from Mr Maund of Bromyard respecting valuing the work & carr: of parcel from him containing his valuation | 0 | 2 | 3 |
| Half a dozen besoms for the school room | 0 | 1 | 3 |
| Incidentals £ | 28 | 10 | 7 |

Total Disbursements — £

State of the Subscriptions
Amount of Annual Subscriptions
Received in advance
Amount to be received

*Expenses incurred in 1816 at the Tenbury National Madras School*

| | |
|---|---|
| coach fares | £3  2s 6d |
| paid to coachmen and guards | 17s 6d |
| expenses on road | 9s 4d |
| seven weeks lodging in London at 5s per week | £1 15s 0d |
| seven weeks living expenses at 14s per week | £4 18s 0d |
| postage of letters | 5s 0d |
| a total of | £11  7s 4d |

The school accommodation consisted of a large room supervised by the schoolmaster who trained the brightest of the older children to act as monitors. They then taught smaller groups of children according to a set system. The master acted as supervisor, examiner and disciplinarian, regularly testing the children, who could be promoted or relegated between the groups according to the extent to which they absorbed knowledge. This system seems incredible today, but it remained common even after 1840. It had the advantage of keeping the teaching staff to a minimum, thus reducing costs, an important consideration when the school's main income was from private donations and scholars' fees, which varied from 1d to 6d per week.

At their meeting on 18 May 1817, the school's committee expressed their delight:

The progress of the children has been considerable allowing for the very backward state in which a large proportion of them have entered the school; the regularity and order of it is such as to afford the best hopes of increased improvement hereafter; the attendance has been good as can be expected during a season of unusual difficulties for the poor; and the increasing applications for Admission are good evidences of the opinion which is generally entertained of the plan ...

The Master was highly commended and awarded a

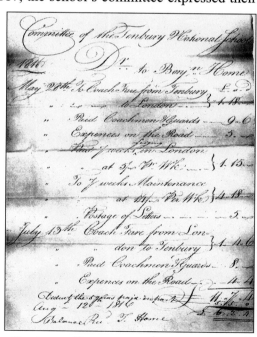

*Benjamin Home's expenses when sent to London to learn how to operate the Madras system of teaching*

gratuity of £5 5s. A room was to be fitted out for 'knitting, sewing and all other female work and Mrs Sarah Evans appointed to instruct them therein'.

By 1829 the Trustees of the school realized the need for better accommodation and they purchased a site in Cross Street from William Holloway for £95. Thomas Hare of Cleobury erected a school building on it for £203 19s plus £18 6s for glazing by Samuel Crane of Teme Street. The cost was met by public subscription plus a donation of £120 from the National Society. The building, now 43-49 Cross Street, came into use on 5 October 1829. By 1830 the school's roll was 114 boys and 56 girls.

The Trustees of the school were all prominent in local affairs: George Rushout Bowles of Burford House; Reverend George Hall, vicar of Tenbury; Reverend T.E. Mytton Holland of Stoke Bliss; Sir Christopher Sydney Smith of Eardiston; Edward Wheeler of Kyrewood; Thomas Yarranton of Tenbury, tanner; and Thomas Blakeway of Tenbury, gentleman. In 1852, William Norris, solicitor and John Laxon Sweet of Tenbury House, surgeon and apothecary, joined the Trustees. William Norris was secretary and treasurer of the school.

In the 1830s and 1840s the school had considerable problems with the shortage of funds and staff turnover. The Master's salary was reduced from £50 to £45 in 1835 and in 1839 to £35. Because of continuing financial difficulties, in 1839 the Master and Matron were dismissed and replacement staff were found at lower salaries. However, it seems that so many incumbents over the next few years left for better paying jobs that the salary offered was soon raised again. Initially Mr and Mrs Stokes were appointed at a joint salary of £55 but in 1840 they left to take up a better job at Kidderminster Union Workhouse. Sam Smith and his wife took up their place at the same salary but were given notice in January 1841 as they were unsuitable and his wife's health was poor.

Over the next five years, a succession of seven individuals or couples held the positions, but were dismissed for a variety of reasons or left for better paid positions. On Mr Pinhorn's appointment in 1855 he was paid £80 on the understanding that his sister acted as matron.

In 1846 the Pupil Teacher System began. Young people aged from about 13 served a five year apprenticeship in a school and were examined each year by Her Majesty's Inspectors (HMIs). They were instructed by the Master in a rigidly structured system outside school hours and they assisted the Master during the school day. If they passed each yearly examination they were given a small stipend and the Master also received a payment from the Government. At the end the apprentices became certified teachers. They then sat an examination for the Queen's Scholarship and if successful were eligible for a place at a training college where they could reach a higher standard. By 1863 Tenbury National School was using pupil teachers on a regular basis.

Also in 1846 the Government gave grants for school management, thus easing the school's financial problems. The grants were based on school numbers, attendance and attainment as judged by HMIs. Additional payments were made for teaching specialist subjects.

In 1854 the Committee decided that a new building was necessary. In 1855 the Cross Street building was replaced by a fine new building in Bromyard

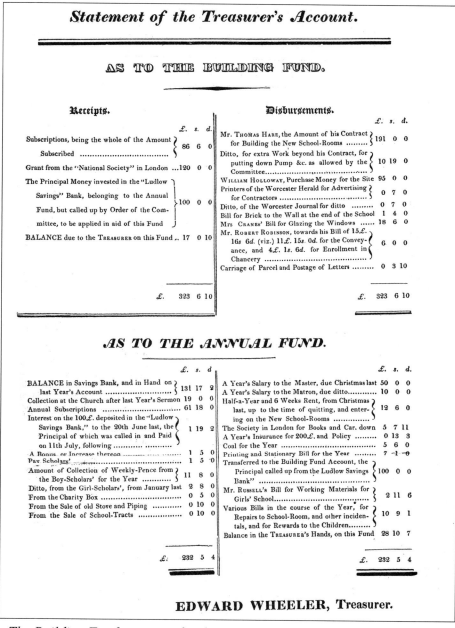

## Statement of the Treasurer's Account.

### AS TO THE BUILDING FUND.

| Receipts. | £. | s. | d. | Disbursements. | £. | s. | d. |
|---|---|---|---|---|---|---|---|
| Subscriptions, being the whole of the Amount Subscribed | 86 | 6 | 0 | Mr. Thomas Hare, the Amount of his Contract for Building the New School-Rooms | 191 | 0 | 0 |
| Grant from the "National Society" in London | 120 | 0 | 0 | Ditto, for extra Work beyond his Contract, for putting down Pump &c. as allowed by the Committee | 10 | 19 | 0 |
| The Principal Money invested in the "Ludlow Savings" Bank, belonging to the Annual Fund, but called up by Order of the Committee, to be applied in aid of this Fund | 100 | 0 | 0 | William Holloway, Purchase Money for the Site | 95 | 0 | 0 |
| | | | | Printers of the Worcester Herald for Advertising for Contractors | 0 | 7 | 0 |
| BALANCE due to the Treasurer on this Fund | 17 | 0 | 10 | Ditto, of the Worcester Journal for ditto | 0 | 7 | 0 |
| | | | | Bill for Brick to the Wall at the end of the School | 1 | 4 | 0 |
| | | | | Mrs Cranes' Bill for Glazing the Windows | 18 | 6 | 0 |
| | | | | Mr. Robert Robinson, towards his Bill of 15£. 16s. 6d. (viz.) 11£. 15s. 0d. for the Conveyance, and 4£. 1s. 6d. for Enrollment in Chancery | 6 | 0 | 0 |
| | | | | Carriage of Parcel and Postage of Letters | 0 | 3 | 10 |
| £. | 323 | 6 | 10 | £. | 323 | 6 | 10 |

### AS TO THE ANNUAL FUND.

| | £. | s. | d | | £. | s. | d. |
|---|---|---|---|---|---|---|---|
| BALANCE in Savings Bank, and in Hand on last Year's Account | 131 | 17 | 2 | A Year's Salary to the Master, due Christmas last | 50 | 0 | 0 |
| Collection at the Church after last Year's Sermon | 19 | 0 | 0 | A Year's Salary to the Matron, due ditto | 10 | 0 | 0 |
| Annual Subscriptions | 61 | 18 | 0 | Half-a-Year and 6 Weeks Rent, from Christmas last, up to the time of quitting, and entering on the New School-Rooms | 12 | 6 | 0 |
| Interest on the 100£. deposited in the "Ludlow Savings Bank," to the 20th June last, the Principal of which was called in and Paid on 11th July, following | 1 | 19 | 2 | The Society in London for Books and Car. down | 5 | 7 | 11 |
| A Bonus, or Increase thereon | 1 | 5 | 0 | A Year's Insurance for 200£. and Policy | 0 | 13 | 3 |
| Pay Scholars' | 1 | 5 | 0 | Coal for the Year | 5 | 6 | 0 |
| Amount of Collection of Weekly-Pence from the Boy-Scholars' for the Year | 11 | 8 | 0 | Printing and Stationary Bill for the Year | 7 | 1 | 0 |
| Ditto, from the Girl-Scholars', from January last | 2 | 8 | 0 | Transferred to the Building Fund Account, the Principal called up from the Ludlow Savings Bank" | 100 | 0 | 0 |
| From the Charity Box | 0 | 5 | 0 | Mr. Russell's Bill for Working Materials for Girls' School | 2 | 11 | 6 |
| From the Sale of old Stove and Piping | 0 | 10 | 0 | Various Bills in the course of the Year, for Repairs to School-Room, and other incidentals, and for Rewards to the Children | 10 | 9 | 1 |
| From the Sale of School-Tracts | 0 | 10 | 0 | Balance in the Treasurer's Hands, on this Fund | 28 | 10 | 7 |
| £. | 232 | 5 | 4 | £. | 232 | 5 | 4 |

**EDWARD WHEELER, Treasurer.**

*The Building Fund accounts for the construction of the new school in 1855*

*The new school built in 1855*

Road at a cost of £999 5s. Much later this building was the study centre for St Thomas More School. It is now a private residence.

In August 1893, the HMI reported:

> The infants are now under the charge of an experienced and skilful teacher and form a separate department. Their work has improved so very considerably that the highest variable grant is recommended. At no distant date the Managers will have to consider the question of funding additional places for the infants. The infants' room is already overfull and the numbers on the books are too large.

The hint was taken and in 1895 a new building was erected for the infants on the opposite side of Bromyard Road at a cost of £760. This building is still in use by Tenbury C. of E. Primary School, the successor to the National School. Other buildings were added later.

The new Infant School was opened in January 1896 with a short dedicatory service. The Rev. D.C. Morris read the prayers and a hymn was sung by the children. In May the Diocesan Inspector reported: 'the infants in their new school are thoroughly well taught. The school is a remarkably good one,' a view endorsed in July by the HMI. But he also said that the higher grant for singing could not be recommended unless there was an improvement.

## School Life

The school logbooks available from 1863 tell of life in the school and give a great deal of detail about education in Tenbury in the 19th century. It is evident that attendance was a major problem, with frequent references to children being absent because their help was required in labour intensive agricultural work such as harvesting, haymaking, bean dropping, potato planting and hop picking. The school had little choice but to accept this, as school attendance was not made compulsory until 1876. Considerable difficulty was experienced in managing the children when they returned as is evident in the logbook entry for 10 July 1865 recorded below. Snow and rain also greatly reduced numbers, with children having to be divested of their wet clothing for drying. Illnesses such as measles, whooping cough, diarrhoea, scarlet fever, mumps and chicken pox also had a serious effect, with the school having to be closed for several weeks during epidemics. Public events also took their toll on attendance with pupils opting for races, cattle fairs, circuses, theatrical performances, foot races, club walks and cricket matches.

When the schoolmaster was a member of the Tenbury battalion of the Worcestershire Volunteers (the forerunner of the Territorial Army) holidays had to be given when he was absent on Volunteer Inspections. In an attempt to improve attendance in 1872, William Norris, a well known town solicitor, offered 6d to each child who attended school 300 times a year and Sunday School 42 days a year. School holidays were from late August to early October for harvesting, a week at Christmas and, later, weeks at Easter and Whitsun.

The school had allotments cultivated by the boys and prizes were regularly awarded for the best. The girls made garments for sale – in 1867 there were shirts at 10d each, night shirts 8d, night gowns 10d, flounced petticoats 6d, nightcaps trimmed 2d and pillow cases 2d per pair. These items could be ordered from the school and were also sold at the Flower Show.

William Norris took a considerable interest in the school, regularly treating the children to such pleasures as visits to Wombwell's Circus and Wild Beast Show, Wombwell's Zoological Temple, Bourn's Russian Circus, Dioramas in the Corn Exchange, slide shows, lectures on electricity and a panorama on Abyssinia. His second wife was a frequent visitor to the school.

Punishments were infrequently recorded, mainly for stealing and truancy. Mr Pinhorn, Master from 1855-75, seemed quite enlightened in his attitude to children. He had an engaging habit of expressing his private thoughts in the logbook. At times he seemed close to despair in his fight against poor attendance and other problems but he invariably soldiered on, as the following entries record:

## 1863

July 27th The same boy again played the truant. The bad behaviour of the child is due to the bad training of his parents. Resolved to do my duty. Punished him.

August 3rd Scarlet fever prevalent. 8 children taken ill. 1 girl died. Prayer offered for the sick. Made a few remarks to the children on the uncertainty of life, the necessity for the preparation for death.

August 23rd Punished a boy for stealing apples. This was the boy punished several times for truant-playing. What shall I do with him? He is quite the pest of his class and the school. He is an example of what bad home discipline produces. I will try kindness. I will pray for him.

October 9th Much pleased with the truthfulness of a scholar. Someone broke a pane of glass. I asked who did it. 'Please sir, I did. I am very sorry. How much is it?' Made a few remarks suited to the occasion.

November 16th Vicar visited and addressed the children on the sin of swearing. The children paid the greatest attention to his impressive address. I hope they will follow his advice. It is strange, but a fact that neither I nor the pupil teachers have heard a single oath or bad word from the children for many months.

November 26th Had great trouble with a very passionate child about 4 years old. After great trouble eventually subdued her without use of the cane. She repented and desired forgiveness.

## 1864

March 21st W. Norris, Esq., our much respected secretary, presented a very handsome football to the boys. They were delighted.

April 4th Superstition has not died out in Tenbury. A girl had a dead spider enclosed in a nutshell suspended from her neck. Her mother had given it to her to protect her from whooping cough.

## 1865

February 11th Found a boy chewing India rubber as he had the toothache.

July 10th I find that the discipline of the school has been greatly impaired by the irregularity of attendance arising from measles, haymaking and wet weather. The remainder of that week was spent paying great attention to the discipline of the school and by Friday it was much improved.

*Schoolchildren and masters at Tenbury School, 1897*

July 18th Punished 7 boys of the first class for bathing in Kyre Brook which flows near the school.

November 22nd Spent a most miserable day in the school. Forty children came wet through and consequently I had to superintend the drying the clothes etc. The room was filled with smoke. We were almost blinded.

There seems to be a gap of about a year from September 1866 when Mr Pinhorn was absent through bad health, his duties being covered by Mr Caldwell, whose logbook entries are more terse.

1867

January A lad being punished for neglecting his lessons. His mother came and bullied me and complained to the vicar who visited the school. [The outcome of the visit is not given.]

May School inspected by Rev. Hernaman HMI who reported that 'the school seems likely to be as efficient under Mr Caldwell as it was under Mr Pinhorn'.

By September Mr Pinhorn was back in post. In April 1869 there is an amusing comment in the report of the Rev. T.A. Smith: 'I should like the children to be able to spell such words as lick her [liquor].'

In September 1875 Mr Pinhorn resigned because of ill health. Mr David Reynolds, certificated teacher, first class, was appointed in his place.

## Goff's School

*Schoolchildren at Tenbury School, c.1935. Tom Powis is second from left in the front row*

As recorded above, Goff's School was founded in 1816 with the support of the Baptists. According to the minutes of the Baptist Chapel, they rented The Steps House adjoining the Bell Inn in Market Street. This is possibly the building presently occupied by the Chinese takeaway. In 1818 the owner of The Steps House died and the executors of his estate gave the Baptists notice to quit. With the help of the Trustees of the Goff estate, they leased a house for the Minister, which also served as a temporary meeting house and school. The Goff Trustees also purchased the site of the Goff's School Building in Cross Street where Tenbury Museum is now housed. The site cost £30 and a meeting house/schoolroom was erected on it for a cost of £100. This building, which is not the present one, opened in 1819.

In 1855 the Baptists erected a chapel at the corner of Cross Street and Berrington Road. Originally a minister's house was attached to it, but it was later demolished to widen the entrance to Berrington Road. The Chapel was funded through donations and a loan of £600 from William Mytton, a farmer of Netherwood. The Baptists ceased to use the chapel in 1948 and it was used as a community centre until 1970, since which time it has had various commercial uses.

At an auction in the King's Head on 23 April 1855 the Baptists purchased the former National School Building in Cross Street for £168 – the date of the completion of the sale was 25 March 1856.

In accordance with the still uneasy public opinion, strict restrictions were laid down for their use of the premises. The purchasers were referred to in the sale indenture as the Society of Protestant Dissenters called the Particular or Calvinist Baptists. The building was to be used as a Sunday or Day School for promoting the unsectarian education of children, in which school the Holy Scriptures were to be used as a daily lesson book. The school could also be used for public meetings and lectures on scientific and benevolent subjects including temperance, peace and anti-slavery. The Trustees of the Goff's

School were then Alfred Heritage, Baptist Minister; Charles Preen of Tenbury, draper; John Foster of Tenbury, currier; William Hyde of Tenbury, glazier; and John Sanders the elder of Hanley William, farmer. In April 1856 they too took a loan of £100 from William Mytton.

For a while the Baptists had three buildings: their new chapel, the former National School and the building on the present museum site. In 1860 they sold the former National School; it is not clear why as there is no reference to either the purchase or the sale in the Chapel minutes. It was purchased by John Foster's daughter, Sarah, for £193 of which £100 was paid to William Mytton in settlement of his loan. Sarah converted the building into the four houses seen today.

In 1863 the Goff's School building on the present museum site was in poor repair and it was demolished to be replaced by the present building, in which Goff's School continued until 1915 when it closed. The Goff's Foundation gave £100 towards the building costs; the rest was met by private donations. Edward Goff has to be admired for his concern for and commitment to the

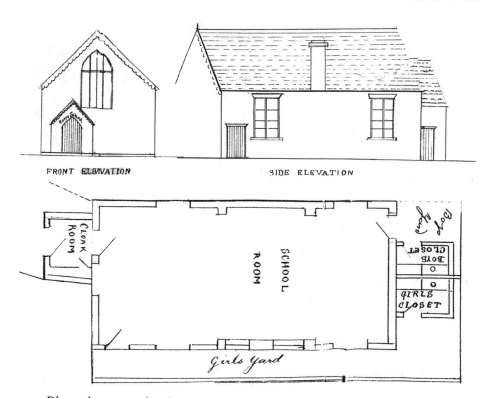

*Plans drawn up for the replacement Goff School in Tenbury in 1863, a building which now houses the museum*

45

education of poor children and, on seeing the charming but tiny building, one has to admire the children as well.

*The entrance to Goff's School, now Tenbury Museum, with from left to right, in the front row: Margaret Stanbridge, Alan Stanbridge, Frank Crisp, Mary Miller and Richard Fox.*
*Middle row: Val Swanick, Margaret Castell, George Price and ?.*
*Back Row: John Greenhill and John Rambaut.*
*All helpers at Tenbury Museum*

# Croquet and Tennis in the Tenbury Area

Tenbury Croquet Club was formed in 1871 and met and held competitions at all the local houses of renown around the Tenbury area. It recorded many of its meetings from its inception to 1875 in a remarkable book of drawings, sketches, photographs and poems. In widely varying artistic styles, using pencil sketches and watercolours, several artists recorded fanciful and factual descriptions of the play, the prizes, the winners and the estates where they met.

About ten matches were played each year between May and September, and venues included Leysters Parsonage, Boraston Rectory, Coreley Rectory, Bockleton Court, Kyrewood House, St Michael's Rectory, Ashford House, Easton Court, Tenbury House on Teme Street (then owned by John Laxton Sweet, a surgeon), Lydiates, Court of Hill, Stoke House, and The Parks in Berrington Road.

The game is a race to get two croquet balls around the circuit of hoops in a prescribed order on a flat grassed lawn. The first player to get through the 12 hoops in the correct order and hit the peg at the end is the winner. The rules were established in 1865 at Chastleton House in Oxfordshire.

The prizes were donated by the members and included items like field glasses, a tea kettle, vases, Indian boxes, a butter dish, a chessboard and a honey pot.

Lawn tennis (as distinct from real tennis which dates from ancient times) was founded by Major Walter Clopton Wingfield, a Welsh army officer, who

*The illustrations on this page and that opposite are taken from a book recording the matches played by Tenbury Croquet Club between 1871 and 1875. Most of the pages contain photographs of the winner and where the matches were played, decorated with drawings and paintings of flowers, leaves and the countryside in general*

devised a set of rules. His game could be played on a lawn or any hard level surface. The court was wider at the baseline than at the middle and the height of the net was 7 feet at each end (now 3 feet 6 inches) and 4 feet 8 inches at the centre (now 3 feet). The new game became popular and Wingfield's rules were soon altered to bring the game closer to its present format. The All England Croquet Club at Wimbledon added the words 'Lawn Tennis' to its title and some grass courts to its croquet lawns. The first championships were held there in 1877 and the Lawn Tennis Association was founded in 1888.

One Tenbury member commented on the change in verse:

*Three of the venues for the croquet matches between 1871 and 1875.*
*Top: Bockleton Hall; Centre: Court of Hill; Lower: Kyrewood House*

When autumn leaves begin to fall,
we put aside the croquet ball:
But let us hope another year;
when summer flowers again appear;
Our friends once more may gather round,
upon the pleasant croquet ground:
That with lawn tennis is now combined,
the club fresh impetus may find;
And under Mrs Hewitt's sway,
may flourish still for many a day.

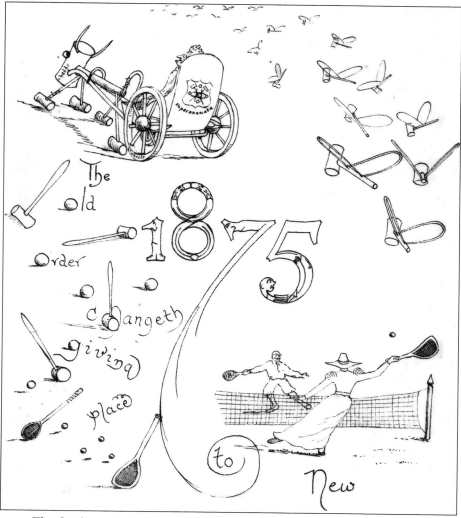

*The final page in the Tenbury Croquet Club book showing the game*
*giving way to tennis*

*Tennis party at The Parklands*

In 1875 the Tenbury Croquet Club followed the example of the All England Croquet Club and introduced lawn tennis. Judging from a cartoon drawn by one of the members, tennis completely displaced croquet, which was depicted as a wheelchair bound geriatric while tennis was represented by an athletic couple. The cartoon bears the caption: 'The old order changeth, giving place to New' (see previous page).

Tennis was later played on the grounds of The Court, the home of the Godson family. This building, demolished in the 1960s, was on the site of the present Greenhill Estate. Public tennis tournaments were held on fete days.

The present Tennis Club probably started playing on the Burgage Courts in the 1930s. It was then known as the Burgage Tennis Club; only later was the name was changed to the Tenbury Tennis Club. The Club now plays throughout the year on three hard surface courts and junior coaching is held on Saturday mornings.

# Stained Glass Windows
# and the Pre-Raphaelites

The East window at St Mary's, Tenbury, is not just handsome, but epitomises the development of stained glass in the Victorian period.

One of the enduring characteristics of this period is the Gothic Revival style which became fashionable in place of the Classical and Regency style of the previous century. Passionately promoting the Gothic Revival was Augustus W.N. Pugin (1812-1852). Shipwrecked at 18, married at 19, widowed at 20, remarried and converted to Roman Catholicism at 21, he branded Classicism as pagan and only Medieval Gothic as true Christian. Pugin designed and restored many churches all over England, involving himself in every aspect of the restoration from furnishings to stained glass.

In time he came into contact with John Hardman (1811-1867), who came from a family business in Birmingham that produced buttons. Hardman formed his own company in 1838 to produce ecclesiastical metalwork in the medieval style. Pugin then produced some of Hardman's designs for candlesticks, brackets, vessels and screens. In 1845 he persuaded Hardman to produce stained glass as Pugin was not satisfied with the work produced by other studios. John Hardman and Company were soon recognised as leading makers in Pugin's Gothic style.

In 1856 Henry Woodyer was the architect chosen by the Rev. Sir Frederick Gore Ouseley for the church and college that he was building at St Michael's near Tenbury. The church is particularly tall, steeply roofed and cruciform and dominates the countryside for a considerable distance. It is lit by many windows in the nave, apse and clerestory for which Woodyer chose John Hardman and Company to provide the stained glass. Hardman produced a series of nave windows illustrating stories in the Bible, and in the eastern apse he designed a magnificent set of tall windows portraying St Michael and 'the heavenly host of angels' in brilliantly coloured glass.

In 1865 Woodyer was chosen to design and supervise the restoration of nearby St Mary's Church in Tenbury Wells. Much of the work was based upon the original Gothic church, with a new organ chamber in Woodyer's steep dramatic style. Again he chose the John Hardman studio for the glass in three new chancel windows. The main five-light east window shown on the rear cover was designed in a very dramatic composition featuring the Ascension of Christ in beautifully balanced colours with delightful angels in the traceries. It compares very well with the windows at St Michael's and is an excellent example of Victorian glass of the period. The Hardman Glass studios are still active in Birmingham today, over 150 years after their founding by John Hardman.

*Stained glass at Rochford church by Morris & Co*

Another local church with a Hardman window is St John the Baptist at Nash, just to the north of Tenbury. This 20th-century window is dedicated to the National Association of Boys Clubs and commemorates the boys' school that occupied Nash Court until 1977. It features a group of boys in various school and sporting activities below a picture of the Good Samaritan.

Thus three churches in the Tenbury area feature work based upon Pugin's passionate promotion of the Gothic Revival style and the leading designers that followed him.

The Tenbury area is also fortunate in having churches with outstanding examples of a totally different style of glass painting. In the 1860s there were many studios in England producing excellent window designs developed from Pugin's discipline of the architectural and historical styles of the medieval period. The demand for windows was so great that many of the commercial firms developed a form of industrial mass production of stained glass.

William Morris (1834-96) and his friends developed a very original and different expression of their fascination with the Middle Ages. Morris and Edward Burne-Jones (1833-98) met at Oxford where they were both studying for a career in the Church. They became very disillusioned with their studies, turned instead to art and became obsessed with the romantic idealism, colour and beauty of the medieval world. Together with Dante Gabriel Rossetti (1828-82), a founder member of the Pre-Raphaelite

*Stained glass at Whitton church by Edward Burne-Jones for Morris & Co*

55

Brotherhood, and the architect Philip Webb (1831-1915), they formed a company in 1861 committed to the medieval ideals of craftsmanship.

At St Michael's Church, Rochford, is an early Morris window of 1863. This east window of three lights contains figurative panels by Burne-Jones and William Morris – an Adoration of the Child and five angels playing musical instruments (see the photograph on p.54). The colours are pastel and the window lets in light through small patterned panels. It is quite a unique window for the period, very fresh and gentle in its effect.

Quite different are the windows by Morris and Company at St Mary's Church, Whitton, a few miles from Tenbury. This is a much later style of the company. Three figures and three scenes from the life of Mary occupy the full height of each light, with a background of foliage and fruit so that there is no clear glass at all (see p.55). This window used existing drawings from the studio with bold and dramatic colouring, a magnificent focus of light in the church.

Rochford and Whitton together form an excellent example of developments in design in the second half of the 19th century. Both windows are outstanding examples of Morris and Company, yet they are totally different in style and composition.

Rochford also has another window but by 'the other William Morris'. William T. Morris (1874-1944) formed a company in London in 1901 called William Morris and Company, which was frequently confused with 'the' Morris and Company that employed Burne-Jones and produced the east windows at Rochford and Whitton. William T. Morris's windows were totally different in style to those of the famous William Morris. Yet Rochford has a window by each of them. The later one, dated 1952, depicts an angel in golden armour with flames around the sword, helmet and legs, a brilliant gleaming figure shown on the front cover, but the very opposite style to the gentle pastel angels by the original William Morris and Burne-Jones in the east window.

The area around Tenbury includes examples of stained glass windows by several leading studios that together illustrate some major developments in the art in the 19th century.

# Roads

Travel was difficult before the 18th century and trade and business took place within local areas, utilising existing waterways, notably the Teme, trackways or old Roman roads.

The first long-distance tracks, called ridgeways or flintways, were created during the Neolithic period and were used to trade flints from which arrow-heads, scrapers and cutters were made. Later, salt was discovered and moved over these and newly created saltways. Many of these routes are still visible in our landscape and some continued to be used as packhorse routes until the 19th century.

The Romans developed a national road system for the rapid movement of troops and goods. Nowhere was this more necessary than in the western Marches and when Ostorius Scapula succeeded Aulus Plautius as Roman governor in AD 47, he moved the frontier westward with campaigns against the Silures of south Wales and the Decangi in the north. Roman engineers built new roadways or redeveloped existing trackways using methods perfected across the Empire. A trench was dug for the bed of the roadway and the bottom covered with a layer of large stones. These were compacted with layers of

*Howard Miller by the remains of a Roman road in Yorkshire*

*Roman ford at Little Hereford*

smaller materials – stones and pebbles mixed with cement – and covered with tight fitting paving stones to form a smooth but cambered surface between kerb stones at the sides which also formed a channel to take away surface water. Roman cement was made with lime produced from burnt limestone in a method used until the 20th century.

Salt was discovered at Droitwich and transported to Leominster on a saltway constructed like this. It is likely that it passed through Great Witley, crossed the Teme at Stanford Bridge and mounted the high ground near Clifton-on-Teme before running along the hilltops to Kyre, Bockleton and Pudleston and on to Leominster. Place names and local oral history provide some evidence of this route: Sallings Common (or Salens Common) suggests a salt connection, and it is recorded that Upper Hamnish is on the site of an old salt road. Stretford suggests a Roman crossing of the Whyle Brook.

Other Roman routes connected encampments on the Brown Clee and Titterstone Clee with Garmsley and Thornbury in a north/south line and may well have crossed the Teme at Tenbury, Burford or Little Hereford, where a ford can still be seen in the river at times of low water.

That a salt link existed between Leomister and Droitwich is reported in the Domesday record in which the entry for Leominster records: 'Woodland 6 leagues long and 3 leagues wide which pays 22s. From these 5s are given to Droitwich for buying timber and 30 measures of salt are had from there.' (In Domesday times, 1 league = 1½ miles.)

After the Romans left, the British and then the Anglo-Saxons used the existing routes, but gradually the network was also extended. Driftways for moving cattle began to connect settlements, whilst the uncultivated strips between ploughed furlongs were first used as walkways to avoid damaging crops and eventually some became permanent roads. This is one theory that may explain why there are so many bends in our present day road system.

With the conquest by the Normans, communication between settlements was improved, although this was more difficult in the Marches because of the terrain. The Anglo-Saxons hired men with horses as messengers, calling them radmen. The term was taken over by the Normans and this may be the source of our term 'road'.

Anglo-Saxon society focussed very much on the family or clan and most travel and trade was within the parish or a small group of parishes. The Normans, however, had a wider outlook on commerce, and sought trade to and from Europe and their homelands. They also soon began to award charters for markets and for fairs to encourage trade.

Markets are likely to have been held unofficially in Tenbury long before a charter was granted to Roger de Clifford by King Henry III in 1249. This grant was for 'one market every week on Tuesday at his Manor of Temettebury, and that they may have one fair every year to continue for two days to wit on the Eve and on the day of the translation of Saint Thomas the Martyr with all liberties and free customs …'.

Charters were granted provided that markets were not nearer to each other than would be required for a man to travel both ways and do his business by daylight. So most market towns are at least 7 miles apart.

To further encourage trade, the Statute of Winchester in 1285 declared that the highways connecting market towns should be widened so that there was no ditch, tree or bush in which a man may lurk to do mischief within 200 feet of each side of the road. Oaks and great beeches were excluded if the ground below the branches were clear.

*King Henry III's seal*

River crossings presented additional hazards and keeping bridges in good repair was costly to whoever owned them. 'Pontage' or a right to collect tolls was therefore often granted – as happened at Eastham bridge. The revenue raised was in part used to maintain the bridge.

Adopting the concept in which the Church allowed the purchasing of indulgences, the upkeep of a bridge could be designated a 'pious meritorious work of God'. An appropriate amount of money for maintenance of the bridge would therefore grant the donor 'remission of punishments after sacramental absolution'.

Hollow-ways used water as one way to clear the road surface. Heavy rain would wash all the surface mud and detritus to the lowest point from where it could be cleared away. During prolonged rain the hollow became a brook, but the system worked well enough for lower lanes except that the roadway sank deeper and deeper between adjacent fields and hedgerows. In around 1810 it was noted that the stag, hounds and huntsmen could quite easily leap over a loaded wagon from one side of a hollow-way to the other, barely noticing the wagon as an obstruction. Unsurprisingly, there were 'lanes full of stones and uphills and down soe steep that with the raines, the waters stood or else ran down the hills which made it exceedingly bad for travelling'.

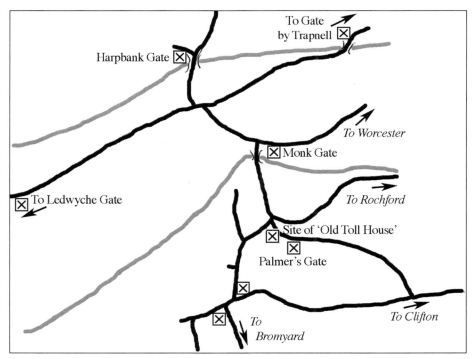

*Map showing the location of Turnpike gates in the vicinity of Tenbury*

As roadways began to be used by people passing through or from other parishes, the question of who was to pay for the work was a contentious one. It was obvious that something had to be done for the sake of trade and commerce and a system of turnpike roads was established

Under this system, a Turnpike Trust would take responsibility for the maintenance of the road or a section of it, in return for charges or tolls paid by users. In 1753 an Act was created 'for surveying, amending, and keeping in repair, the said roads in and near to the Town of Tenbury'. Trustees were empowered to '… erect a gate or gates, turnpike or turnpikes, toll house or toll houses in, upon, cross or on the side of any part of the said road and shall demand … the tolls and duties …'. As a result ten turnpike roads were established in the Tenbury area which operated between about 1760 and 1870.

The Act prescribed the following charges:

| | |
|---|---|
| for every carriage drawn by 4 or more horses | 1s 0d |
| for every carriage drawn by 4 or more oxen or two oxen with one or more horses | 1s 0d |
| for every carriage with one, two or three horses | 6d |
| and for every mule, horse or ass laden or unladen | 1d |
| for every drove of oxen, cows or meat cattle | 1s 6d per score |
| and so in proportion for any greater or less number | |

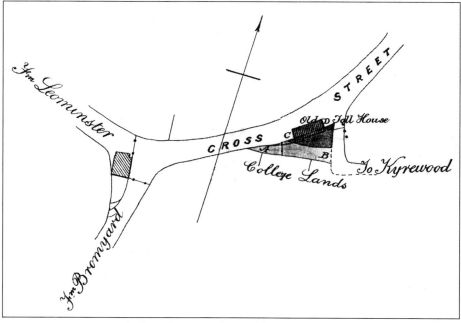

*A plan showing the 'Old Toll House',*
*the site of which is marked on the map opposite*

| Date | Day | £ | s | d |
|---|---|---|---|---|
| 5 | Friday | 0 | 2 | 8 |
| 6 | Satturday | 0 | 3 | 0 |
| 7 | Sunday | 0 | 3 | 1 |
| 8 | Munday | 0 | 1 | 7 |
| 9 | Tuesday | 0 | 5 | 7 |
| 10 | Wednesday | 0 | 8 | 0 |
| 11 | Thursday | 0 | 2 | 8 |
| 12 | Friday | 0 | 1 | 7 |
| 13 | Satturday | 0 | 0 | 10 |
| 14 | Sunday | 0 | 2 | 4 |
| 15 | Munday | 0 | 0 | 11 |
| 16 | Tuesday | 0 | 2 | 0 |
| 17 | Wednesday | 0 | 0 | 5 |
| 18 | Thursday | 0 | 0 | 9½ |
| | Ex.Ns | 1 | 13 | 5½ |

19 Recd the above p Wm Hall

| Date | Day | £ | s | d |
|---|---|---|---|---|
| 19 | Friday | 0 | 0 | 4 |
| 20 | Satturday | 0 | 0 | 6 |
| 21 | Sunday | 0 | 1 | 0 |
| 22 | Munday | 0 | 1 | 7 |
| 23 | Tuesday | 0 | 1 | 10 |
| 24 | Wednesday | 0 | 1 | 10½ |
| 25 | Thursday | 0 | 0 | 2 |
| 26 | Friday | 0 | 5 | 4½ |
| 27 | Satturday | 0 | 1 | 6 |
| 28 | Sunday | 0 | 2 | 2 |
| 29 | Munday | 0 | 2 | 2 |
| 30 | Tuesday | 0 | 4 | 4 |
| Octbr 1 | Wednesday | 0 | 2 | 6 |
| 2 | Thursday | 0 | 2 | 5 |
| | Ex.Ns | 1 | 8 | 9 |

3 Recd the above p Wm Hall

| Date | Day | £ | s | d |
|---|---|---|---|---|
| Octbr 3 | Friday | 0 | 1 | 1 |
| 4 | Satturday | 0 | 0 | 6 |
| 5 | Sunday | 0 | 0 | 4 |
| 6 | Munday | 0 | 0 | 4 |
| 7 | Tuesday | 0 | 2 | 2 |
| 8 | Wednesday | 0 | 1 | 9 |
| 9 | Thursday | 0 | 0 | 6 |
| 10 | Friday | 0 | 2 | 7 |
| 11 | Satturday | 0 | 0 | 8 |
| 12 | Sunday | 0 | 0 | 5 |
| 13 | Munday | 0 | 0 | 5 |
| 14 | Tuesday | 0 | 0 | 2 |
| 15 | Wednesday | 0 | 0 | 6 |
| 16 | Thursday | 0 | 0 | 7 |
| | Ex.Ns | 0 | 14 | 2 |

17 Recd the above p Wm Hall

| Date | Day | £ | s | d |
|---|---|---|---|---|
| 17 | Friday | 0 | 1 | 2 |
| 18 | Satturday | 0 | 0 | 5 |
| 19 | Sunday | 0 | 2 | 0½ |
| 20 | Munday | 0 | 2 | 2 |
| 21 | Tuesday | 0 | 1 | 6 |
| 22 | Wednesday | 0 | 2 | 9 |
| 23 | Thursday | 0 | 1 | 2 |
| 24 | Friday | 0 | 0 | 5 |
| 25 | Satturday | 0 | 0 | 10 |
| 26 | Sunday | 0 | 1 | 4 |
| 27 | Munday | 0 | 1 | 4 |
| 28 | Tuesday | 0 | 0 | 4 |
| 29 | Wednesday | 0 | 0 | 7 |
| 30 | Thursday | 0 | 0 | 8 |
| 31 | Friday | 0 | 0 | 4 |
| Nobr 1 | Satturday | 0 | 0 | 3 |
| 2 | Sunday | 0 | 0 | 9 |
| 3 | Munday | 0 | 2 | 0 |
| 4 | Tuesday | 0 | 0 | 11 |
| 5 | Wednesday | 0 | 0 | 11 |
| 6 | Thursday | 1 | 1 | 5½ |
| | Ex.Ns | 0 | 14 | 2 |
| | | 1 | 15 | 5 |

7 Recd the above p Wm Hall

*Turnpike gate accounts for Tenbury drawn up 'For Wm Pateshall'*

| for every drove of calves and hogs | 6d per score |
| and so in proportion for any greater or less number | |
| and for every drove of sheep and lambs | 5d per score |
| and so in proportion for any greater or less number | |

Pedestrians did not have to pay and no charges were made on election days.

The trustees were responsible for all maintenance, for the hiring of toll keepers, and the erection of milestones.

Not surprisingly, turnpikes were not universally popular but were most notably disliked by those who had to move farm stock. In 1735 an armed mob pulled down a gate at Ledbury; two people were killed and the keeper threatened. But the system served its purpose until duties were taken over by the Tenbury Highway Board in 1870.

In 1784 Mail Coach services were begun and relied heavily on a satisfactory road system. Under a risk of paying 40 shillings, pikemen had to have the gates on the turnpike roads open and ready for the Mail Coach to pass through free of charge. But Mail Coaches also brought highwaymen or robbers and there was an odd quirk of the law that favoured highwaymen. It stated that if a man fell victim to a highwayman when travelling on the Sabbath there was no redress in law.

Crossroads were often places of execution and where suicides were buried. In the hope of preventing those buried at crossroads from rising to do further evil, stakes were said to have been driven through their hearts. Locally, places with names such as Callows Grave, Gallows Bank and Weeping Cross may indicate such burial places. This practice ended in 1823 when an Act of Parliament forbade such burials and required the setting aside of unconsecrated ground by the churchyard for the burial of unhallowed corpses.

*The site of the old coach road between Tenbury and Bromyard*
*on the top of Haws Hill running across the picture*

Tenbury Turnpike Tolls

To Be Let

Notice is hereby given, That the TOLLS arising at the several Toll-gates upon the 'TENBURY TURNPIKE ROADS,' LEADING FROM Tenbury to the Clee Hill, and also towards Bromyard, and over the Old Wood, and the Raddle Bank, towards Leominster, in the counties of Salop, Worcester and Herefords, and called 'Stockton Gate', 'Tenbury Gate', 'Harp-Bank Gate', 'Knowle Gate', 'Bennett's-End Gate', and Berrington-Lane Gate', will be LET by AUCTION to the best Bidder, at the Swan Inn, in the parish of Burford, in the county of Salop, (near to the town of Tenbury) on Thursday, the 20th day of March next, at a Meeting of the Commissioners, to be then and there for that purpose held, between the hours of eleven and three o'clock of the same day, for any term not exceeding three years, as the Commissioners then present shall determine, commencing at Lady-day, 1828, in manner directed by the several Acts now in force, 'For Regulating Turnpike Roads'. Which Tolls produced the last year the sum of 450s, above the expenses of collecting them, and will be put up that sum, Whoever happens to be the best Bidder, must, at the same time, pay One Month in advance of the Rent at which such Tolls may be Let, and give Security, with sufficient Sureties, to the satisfaction of the Trustees, for the payment of the remainder of the Rent in advance, Monthly.

Notice is hereby also Given, that at the said Meeting New Trustees will be elected in the room of those deceased.

JAMES ROBINSON
Clerk to the Trustees of the said Turnpike Roads.

Tenbury 11th February 1828

*An advertisement placed in* Berrows Worcester Journal, *28 February 1828*

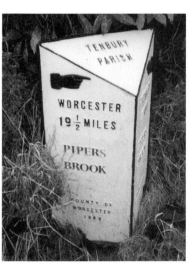

The network of roads in this country has a long history and it is through the engineering skill and financial risk of many who created and maintained them that we have them to use, or overuse, today.

*One of the milestones*
*that survives in Tenbury parish*

# Tenbury Bridge

Tenbury Bridge is bent in the middle. It causes traffic problems and creates frustration and courtesy in equal measure, and it came about because of the weather.

Before 10,000 BC the Teme River flowed in the other direction towards Woofferton, through Leominster to the River Wye. Glacial action formed a bank of earth south of Woofferton which is still there today. This dammed the Teme and caused the formation of Woofferton Lake. The pressure of the water eventually caused the Teme to burst through at Knightwick and join the Severn, so creating the present river.

Rivers were the motorways of pre-medieval times and so were well travelled by boat or on paths along the banks. Crossing rivers was done at fords or where this was not possible by elementary bridges. Floods therefore caused considerable disruption.

After the Norman Conquest, Tenbury found itself on the main road from Worcester to Ludlow and from Bewdley to Aberystwyth. The main market area of Tenbury led from the market square (actually a triangle) at the end of Church Street, called All Hallows Street at the time, to the river. Any early bridge (of which no trace remains) aligned with Church Street. In the 13th century burgage plots were created along Teme Street and the focus of the town moved from Church Street. As the three northern stone arches align more with Church Street than Teme Street it is possible that they or their foundations are from before this time.

Originally, the Teme River bent in a horseshoe shape around Castle Tump and this was the old Worcestershire/Shropshire boundary that was marked on maps as late as 1900. About 1580 a flood caused the Teme to break through the horseshoe and take its present course. This meant that three southern arches had to be added to the bridge to align with the new direction of the river and Teme Street as the new main thoroughfare of the town. This was a wooden bridge on stone piers. It necessitated a bend in the bridge that has been preserved since then. The county boundary remained in the centre of the bridge – the northern arches belong to Shropshire and the southern to Worcestershire.

*Large timbers found in the River Teme in 1986 near The Peacock Inn. The largest measured 50ft x 22in square*

A later flood in 1615 again damaged the bridge and the timbers were lost. In 1986 several large timbers were rescued from the Teme downstream from Tenbury and taken to the Avoncroft Museum of Buildings at Bromsgrove. The timbers were dendrochronologically dated, with a growth period beginning in 1371 and a felling between 1590 and 1595. It is very likely therefore that these massive timbers were part of the early medieval bridge and they can be seen at the museum.

Repairing the bridge often put huge financial strains on local resources. A note at the Worcester Quarter Sessions in 1615 records: 'Pray that adjoining parishes be ordered to contribute towards the repair of a great stone bridge and a wooden bridge over [the] river Teme damaged by the sudden flood of water about middle of March last – the cost of repairs will be very great amounting to £30 and as it is the great thoroughfare from most places of Wales to the Citie of London.' Tenbury Bridge was ordered to be repaired, at least that part of it in Worcestershire. Shropshire would have to repair the northern part.

In 1814 Thomas Telford surveyed the structure. As the *Tenbury Wells Advertiser* was to report many years later, on 14 November 1871, he found the bridge to be only 12 feet wide and taking an ever increasing amount of traffic. However it only allowed 'one vehicle to pass at a time and no footway with little triangular recesses at each pier for the foot passengers to retire into when meeting a vehicle. An adventurous pedestrian, despising these cities of refuge, assayed to pass a wagon load of barley and was crushed to death between wheel and wall.' He proposed widening it to 16 feet with the use of cast iron arch ribs.

On 21 April 1814, Robinson & Wheeler, Clerk to the Commissioners of the Tenbury Turnpike Trust, put the following notice in the *Tenbury Advertiser*:

Notice is hereby given, that all thoroughfare over the said Bridge, (except for Foot Passengers) will be stopt in the month of May next, during the repairs of the said Bridge; and that in lieu thereof, all Persons must cross the Ford over the River Team [*sic*], on the right-hand side of the Tenbury end of the said Bridge, which will be properly fenced and made safely passable for all Waggons, Carts, Carriages, Horses and Cattle.

Whilst the subsequent repair work was underway, the Press Gang often came to look for lively young men for the army and navy, but could never find any in Tenbury. The men working on the bridge were always warned of their approach, and when the Press Gang appeared, the only persons to be seen about the bridge were reportedly women and cripples.

Telford had recommended that the bridge be widened to 16 feet. As the *Advertiser* so belatedly reported, 'The improvement has been accomplished mainly on the Girder principle. Three arches on the Town side have been built,

*Repairs in its present form*

1st — To lower the point of Waste Ground above the Bridge on the Tenbury side to near the level of low water

2 — Instead of replacing Causeways between the Arches near Tenbury, which always would cause an Overfall, to underbuild the Piers to a proper depth under water, with Ashlers laid in British Cement, to admit of the surface of the Bed adjacent to the Piers being protected by the Sand and Gravel, like the other parts of the Bed of the River —

3 — To repair the foundations of all the other Piers & Abutments with Ashlers & British Cement, remove the trees & other Vegetables, repair the Piers, Abutments, Arches & Spandrels by taking out & replacing the decayed & injured Masonry & pointing the whole —

4 — To point all the Parapets, & replace such parts of the Coping as is decay'd with new Stone.

5 — To pave the whole Roadway with pebble Stones of a proper size.

6 — To cut off a few Yards from the corner of the Field adjacent to the Inn in order to render that turning commodious & safe, & continue a Coat of as the present, is capable of, And would cost

The Shropshire part — 100.12.6
Worcestershire Do — 483.5.6
£503.18.0

*Part of Thomas Telford's report on the necessary repairs to the bridge in 1814*

67

*An engraving showing the bridge, c.1780*

*Notice seeking further subscriptions to allow the work that was carried out in 1868 to proceed*

giving the necessary width at this point, from thence from pier to pier across the stream spring light but strong wrought iron girders, three feet deep, firmly secured to the piers head, on which are laid the bearers for the corrugated iron covering the whole, bolted firmly together and to the old work; on this are laid several inches of concrete; then the usual metal on the roadway, then pavement, a fluted rail laid across the facing gives an appropriate finish to this part of the work.'

In 1841 further repairs were carried out, when 'A rate of one farthing in the pound on all rateable property within the hundred of Doddingtree (upper and lower division) [was] raised and paid to T.H. Davis the Bridgewarden for the repair of Bridges within the said hundred of Doddingtree:

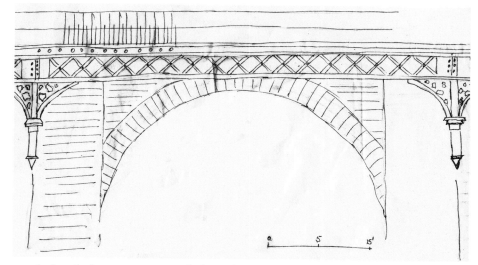

*A sketch that accompanied plans for the widening of the bridge in 1868*

Upper Division   43 – 18 - 2 ¾
Lower Division   39 –   8 - 0 ¾
The whole       83 –   6 – 3 ½'

The bridge was widened again to 23' 6" in 1868. Guarantees for the work were given by E.V. Wheeler, S.H. Godson, Mr Norris and Mr Bingham for the

*Tenbury Bridge in 1905*

remainder of the cost not raised by public subscription or appeals to Worcester County who 'considered Tenbury too far obscure to warrant the funds'.

In 1908 it was further widened and strengthened with reinforced concrete. The bridge is now a Grade I listed structure and still has the bend in the middle.

# Ice Houses

Tenbury has some hidden treasures. At one time ice houses were commonplace and in daily use. Now they are broken, filled in, covered with leaves and ivy and all but invisible under saplings and mature trees.

In a time when all food was seasonal and produced on site or locally in the Teme Valley, the preservation of perishable food was very important before the development of canning and freezing. Also, the ability to serve summer ices was the sign of a very sophisticated household indeed!

The colder climate of the 1800s meant that ice was common in winter, so large brick-lined ice houses were built as an inverted cone-shape in a pit dug into the shaded side of a hill or mound near a pond or river where the ice could be harvested. They were large constructions, designed to hold a two years' supply.

Entrances were on the north in the earliest ice houses, just below the point where the roof joined the walls, but it was found that an entrance on the south-east was beneficial so that the morning sun would evaporate the damp. It was important to keep ice dry as water conducts heat. A sloping drain from the bottom of the pit carried meltwater into a nearby pond or river. Large ice houses had long zig-zag tunnel entrances with heavy insulated doors at each end to prevent warm air blowing directly into the pit.

More modest establishments built timber and thatched ice houses, again over a pit in the ground. Drainage was by either a drain or through a layer of spruce boughs covered with boards. Alternatively, they may have been as simple as a pit filled with ice covered by excavated soil.

The properties of insulation were applied to ice houses more readily than to houses and so cavity walls, timber stud walls, ventilation, waterproofing and the control of damp were techniques used. Straw was used on the bottom and sides of the ice and sometimes in between layers of the ice to slow down the rate of melting. Where straw was not plentiful, reeds, sawdust or timber were used.

Ice was then removed when required and transported to the house for use in the kitchen, dairy, larder and brewery. There may also have been a larder built alongside the ice to take advantage of the cold air and preserve foods not requiring such low temperatures.

Collecting the ice was dangerous and difficult. On many estates there was an artificially created ice pond or well, fed by a small stream or spring. This was constructed as one or more large shallow brick lined boxes 3 feet or more deep. They may have been as large as a quarter or half an acre in area. Water was allowed in, skimmed to clear it of leaves and debris and left to freeze. Top flooding was allowed each evening to build up a good thickness. This was known as icing! Once frozen it was cut out and transported to the ice house during the evening and night when temperatures were at their lowest.

In other places, natural or larger lakes or ponds were harvested when the ice was 2 or 3 inches thick. It was cut into strips a foot or so wide, by long handled mallets. The rest was smashed into fist-sized chunks, salvaged by long handled sieves and taken to the ice house. Here it was dropped in through a hole in the top and rammed down to make huge solid blocks which melted less quickly than ice containing air. A cartwheel was often used to cover the drain and stop the ice from falling in. When ice was in short supply, snow could be treated in the same way.

In the brief time when the ice house was empty – usually mid autumn – all rotten timber or brush from the bottom of the pit was removed, the drain cleared, and new flooring and insulation put in; the brickwork was checked and

*Members of Tenbury Archaeology Group clearing the ice house at Kyrewood in 1991. It is believed that this ice house was built in c.1850*

*Looking out through the entrance of the Kyrewood ice house during its clearing out in 1991*

*A surviving ice house in the grounds of Powis Castle, Shropshire*

limewashed if necessary. The roof brickwork or thatch was repaired and the door seals checked.

By the 19th century ice was gathered in the Arctic Circle and shipped to Britain and thence on to the Midlands by railway. With the lack of manpower at the end of the Great War, the development of iceboxes and subsequently refrigerators powered by electricity, ice houses became redundant and they quietly crumbled away.

# Fanny Griffin

The *Tenbury Wells Advertiser* for 21 October 1939 included the following notice:

> Miss Fanny Griffin died Sunday, October 15th 1939. Born in Tenbury in an old black and white house, recently pulled down, near the church, which she loved and was a regular worshipper for years.
>
> After her father's death she, her mother and brothers and sister moved to the Bath's cottage, and at the time of the great flood in May 1886 were in great peril of being washed away, being marooned for a day and a half with no one to hear their cries for help. A few years ago Miss Griffin wrote, and gave to some of her friends, a picturesque account of her early life and some of the happenings of old Tenbury days.

It is these reminiscences that follow.

My mother's maiden name was Ann Barnett. She was born at Rochford and went to Rochford school and was servant maid at Mrs W. Nickles' farm, Kyre Wood, where I have been told she met John Griffin, a very old man. Her friends told her she would repent it marrying an old man like that. She told them it was better to be an old man's darling than a young man's slave. The wedding came off between them and the first house they lived in after they were married was one of those cottages at the Brook Kyre Wood. My brother George was born there, and Alfred, and my little sister Elizabeth. They moved from the Brook and went to a house at the Old Wood in Tenbury parish and that was where I was born. … then they moved house again and went to live at a house in Church Street … and that was where my father died.

My brother George went to the Tenbury National School and when he left he was put to the shoe making for ten years. Mr Godson, this present Mr Godson's grandfather, paid for the apprenticeship and he learned his trade with Mr Handley. My brother Alfred I don't know much about as he wasn't at home with us. He used to be out at service till the last twenty years or so. He came home and worked on Kyre Wood farm and lived with us and his ten shillings a week which he paid us for his lodgings helped us as my brother George's work was nothing to depend on. My sister Elizabeth wasn't able to earn anything. She was a very good kind sister and done all she could. She used to do all the light housework and the bit of cooking and the sewing and mending and was very thoughtful for me. She knew how hard I was working.

## Washing for St Michael's

After my father died, my mother went out charring and washing and went out nursing with Dr Sweet. She nursed Mrs Banfield with all her children but the oldest. After a while, Mrs Banfield got my mother the washing from St Michael's College; the housekeeper and

*Fanny Griffin*

five maid servants and two page boys and all the surplices from the Church we done for fifteen years. My brother George used to fetch and take it. That was two journeys a week. He used to take and fetch it in a wheelbarrow.

When my mother had all that washing from St Michael's College she used to have a woman to wash a day and half a day … as we couldn't do it all ourselves when we had the surplices, which was three times year. The whole set was thirty-six. We got eight pence each for the surplices … They were so long, not short like they are now, and very dirty round the bottom of them. The housekeeper, Miss Hill – we also done her washing. We had hers every fortnight. … We had two page boys. There was five maid servants which allowed fifteen shillings a quarter for each girl and twelve shillings a quarter for the two page boys each. It was very dirty washing and some weeks we used to have seventy-two aprons from five maids. My mother done it for fifteen years.

## The Flood of 1886

We lost that [washing] work in the big flood 1886. … My dear mother was very brave through it all. She said all day somebody will come. We shan't be here another night. She had got good faith. My brother Alfred said when he called to us from the hedge at the front of the house, if he hadn't no answer he told us he should have jumped over the hedge. … No mistake, we were in great peril all one night and a day. We burnt a light all night. Things aren't so bad but what it might be much worse if it had been in the short days … It began to get light soon after four o'clock and broad daylight at eight o'clock when we could see.

Our rooms were all on one floor and the house was full of water at ten o'clock at night and under our bedrooms there was a cellar with six feet of water. It was on a Thursday night as the house was full of water and we huddled on the bed. My brother George stood on a chair at the foot of the bed. We had nothing to

*The Teme bridge in floodwater, top in 1899, lower in 1924*

*Teme Street in 1924*

*Market Street in 1961*

eat nor drink for about twenty-four hours. About eight o'clock on Friday night we heard voices coming. It was Mr Barnes and Mr Mitten come with a boat to take us away. They boated us all up the Crow Yard right into Market Street where they had many cheers to see the boat landed safe.

## Family Life

We was a very happy family. We never quarrelled with each other and my brothers Alfred and George were both very steady. They never smoked nor drank. After the big flood in 1886 my mother commenced to go very feeble. We left Bath cottage after a while … for one in Scotland Yard, Church Street. It was a very small cottage but we was afraid after what we went through there in the flood. By this time my mother got much worse – not able to be about at all. Dr Ross said what she was suffering was from creeping paralysis and softness of the brain. She was quite invalid for ten years. We had to feed and do all for her like a baby. My sister Elizabeth was living then and was able to help me nurse her.

Suddenly, my sister Elizabeth was taken ill with pneumonia. She was only ill a week. It was on a Saturday afternoon she passed away. I left Mrs Warrel, a neighbour, with her while I

*Two views of cottages in Church Street flooded in 1910*

*Market Street in 1901*

went to do my dusting at the Church. Never thought when I left she was so near death and a boy came to me in the Church and told me I was to go home at once and when I get home I found she was gone.

## Church Work

When my brother George and myself had the Church work we had to carry the water from where we could. Mr Ross proposed the water laid on for the use of the Church. It wasn't done. But a few years after it was laid on, Vicar Eliot got very dissatisfied about things. He told us from the pulpit as there was five men and one woman doing what one man and one woman should do and he was determined to have a change.

These were the five: Mr Dadge, Clerk, my brother George Griffin, vesper [verger?], Tom Beb – he used to dig the graves – Tom Squires, organ blower, Davis the florist done the Church Yard Cross and the flower borders and I cleaned it. My brother rang the bell and we had five fires going in the winter and two and three rings every day.

At the vestry meeting … soon after, the Vicar commenced to work to get this man and his wife and put we out. I sent a letter in which I … explained all the work my brother and I done. This was done [and] the letter was read to the meeting. Mr Norris asked how they been [getting] all that work for three and nine pence a week. The Vicar said Fanny Griffin. Mr Norris said she haven't been doing a man's work, attending five fires and ringing the bell and lighting up the Church?

Before the Vicar got anyone else to do the Church work he [Mr Norris] came and asked me if I would do it. This was decided at the meeting that they would pay me five shillings a week. The Vicar came his self to ask me. I said I would accept your kind offer and I done it for about two years for this five shillings. My brother wasn't able to help me with the Church work then.

Then the days we used to have the Church work there was morning and evening prayer daily and on Saints' days three services and we were supposed to ring the bell till the Vicar came down the Chancel robed. He was always very unpunctual [and] he was cross if we left off ringing the bell till he came down.

Rev. Thomas Ayscough Smith was vicar of Tenbury Parish Church for six years … and when it came out they was leaving, I said to him how sorry I was to hear that you was leaving. No, he said, it was such a very kind offer from the Bishop that he could not refuse it. There was a subscription made for him by we parishioners and what was bought for them was a very nice standing lamp. The time [for the presentation] was made known for the people to meet at the Corn Exchange. I remembers well it was in the month October. Mr Preston the lawyer, Mount Cottage, Tenbury was presenting the lamp up on the platform. He hadn't said but a very few words [when] he suddenly fell headlong off the platform, lamp and all in the presence of all the people. The dear vicar went with haste to take the very sad news to Mrs Preston. The maid told me Minnie Taylor said as Mrs Preston said to the vicar, 'Is the fall fatal?' … He said, 'Quite fatal.' …

[In] years gone by we have in our parish church these big box seats. My brother remembered them. You couldn't see the people in them. My brother used to say the people used to go to sleep and snore and Beadle Rantons used to go about the church with a long black stick with a knob at the end and look over the pews when this snoring commenced and nobble him with this stick.

## In Service

When [I] was in service at the Rev. Brone, Eastham Rectory, there were four of us: Mrs Owens was the cook. She was a Welsh woman. Jane Henges was the housemaid. She was Mrs Kelley's sister. Ernest Mapp was the groom and I, Fanny Griffin, was the kitchen maid.

I had a very good place, plenty of good bread and cheese and roasted beef. The cook used to make some jolly good roly poly puddings. Mrs Owens always lit the kitchen fire herself.

The old girl always called me Martha. When it is time to get up … she had to pass our bedroom [and] she would open the door and say, 'Are thees up Martha? It is time to get up now.' That would be about seven o'clock. She was going down then. Jane had got to be down about half past seven to take Mrs Brone a cup of fine tea made with milk and the Master a cup of tea which the cook got ready for her to take them. The Rev. Brone, his wife was a very good master and mistress. The kitchen at the Rectory was a very big old fashioned one with those big old fashioned flags … To whiten them round the edges the old girl, Mrs Owens, used to say, 'Lassie, it is too much for thee to do in one day.' I had to do the one half on a Friday and the other half on Saturday.

[There] was also a big old fashioned fire place at the Eastham Rectory, now called Robin's End. The Rev. Brone used to have dinner at half past seven in the evenings. He very often had Dr Sweet and Dr Murray to dinner with them. Ernest Mapp used to wait at table.

We always had prayers at ten o'clock. They would ring the bell from the room. That was for Jane to go and put the chairs ready. Mrs Owens, the cook, was first and then Jane, then [me] Fanny and Ernest. We used to go in very reverent and take our places. The master read the prayers. He used to read them so reverent.

When I left after my twelve months Rector Brone said he would give me a character as would take me to any gentleman's place. I didn't go to service after I was eighteen years of age. I stayed at home and helped my mother …

## At Kyrewood

My brother Alfred Griffin, when he worked at Kyrewood Farm, Tenbury, the money he had was fourteen shillings a week. All the workmen had fifteen shillings three times a year which they called harvest money. Then again they had task work and used to let them have a horse and cart in the winter to fetch a load of coal from the pits, Mamble … The Master use to let them have the horses and carts in the winter when there wasn't much work about.

## The Church Organ

Some years ago … Mr Godson gave this organ as is in our church. They decided to bring it down out of the gallery and put it in the present place where it is now. Mr Curson, Tenbury, was the architect [sic, it was actually Henry Woodyer] and Mr Hewitt, Tenbury, was the builder. One day when I was in the church at my work, I heard very loud words with the architect and Mr Hewitt. … Mr Curson was very angry [and] that was the last time he paid a visit to see the building going on. Mr Curson was taken ill and in a very short time died – in the middle of the building [work]. If he had lived he would have had it down again.

What a handsome present to give our little parish church and I think it very nice to have one of the family living with us in Tenbury and that is Esq Godson, one of the grandsons.

My brother George was organ blower when the organ was in the gallery for many years. Mr Thomas, the printer, Teme Street, Tenbury was organist at the time. My brother was also one of the bell ringers.

Mr Bishop, Bromyard Road, said as my brother was organ blower when he was a boy in the choir and he said as when Vicar Ayscough Smith had concluded his sermon and the amen was wanted, the organist, Mr Thomas put his hands on the keys [but] could get no answer. … he went round to see what had happened. The organ blower was gone to sleep.

About twenty years ago there was a ghost seen in the parish church. Mr Howard, the organist was taking the boys in the chancel for their practice. They were all … hard at it. The body of the church [was] all in darkness and the chancel lit up. The boys on the vicar's side suddenly stopped singing and one said, 'Please to look there. ... It's the vicar.' But no vicar appeared.

It reappeared ... and the organist saw it and went to the place where it dispersed. He said he felt a bit nervous, [but] to satisfy the boys he went. It would look very particular in the dark church. It brought the practice to a close and they all left and locked the ghost in the church. The boys wouldn't go to the church for their practice for some weeks after.

## The Fullers

The late Mrs Fuller, Tenbury, and Mr Fuller years ago used to be at the general post office, Tenbury Wells. Mr Fuller was postmaster for some years and then he resigned as postmaster and took to the advertising and printing business in Tenbury. Mr Fuller was a very nice man and liked by all in Tenbury. He was a churchwarden for some years. He had a serious operation and was very ill after and died. They had one son. He was clever with music. He was organist at several different places about. At last he went to China.

[His mother] went to live at a private house. She was there some years [and] I used to go there to work every Saturday afternoon from two o'clock till about six o'clock – all kitchen work – work that I liked. I was very poorly paid but every sixpence helped.

When Mrs Fuller died about eighteen months ago, she left me ten pounds in her will. It was very kind of Mrs Fuller to think of me [and] it was a little recompense back for what I did for her some years past. It will be very helpful to me.

When I, Fanny, and my brother George Griffin took to the work at our parish church, if we were poorly paid, we couldn't give our labour to a better place. I had kind friends at the time – one was respected. Everything is altered now. Church work isn't like it used to be when the Griffins was caretakers of it. Myself and my dear brother George was doing something there every day. We done the work at it for six and twenty years.

There's no one living now as can tell as much about them days. It was all so old fashioned times.

In *Tenbury – Some Record of its History*, Miss M.S. Joyce notes that Mrs Griffin was 'a very fine character, a clever charming old woman. Her husband had been confirmed a cripple and died when the children were young. There were two sons and two daughters, all more or less afflicted. George had a large patch of white hair among his otherwise very dark locks. This is known, of course, to be an omen of death by drowning. The Griffins were much respected. Indeed their whole history may well be regarded as a true romance of a humble life, faithful service unnoticed, too often ill-rewarded. For thirty-four years, at a weekly wage of 3s 9d between them, George Griffin and his sister Fanny cleaned Tenbury Church, dusted it, rang the bell, and did all the odd jobs in it. On Sundays George would sit in the church clad in an old cassock given him by one of the vicars.'

In a transcribed memoir of 1994, Mr Caldicott remembers burying Fanny Griffin. He also recalled that she had about 80 warts on her face, spoke as though she had no roof to her mouth, and that she kept house for Nobs (Mr Snobs the shoemaker in Cross Street). One day a man reputedly came to her and asked for a pair of shoes. She said, 'You should know better than coming here on a Sunday asking for shoes.'

'I have the money in my hand for them.'

'In that case come on in!' she said.

# William Norris, Man of Tenbury

Few people can have had as great an impact on the Tenbury district as William Norris. For more than half of 19th century he played an important role in virtually every aspect of the town's life, working almost until the day of his death.

Born in 1821, he was the youngest son of Rev. T. Norris, vicar of Harby in Leicestershire. He was admitted as a solicitor in 1842 having served his articles with Mr White of Grantham. After a period in Newport, Isle of Wight, in the firm of Sewell, Escourt and Norris, he came to Tenbury in 1849, succeeding to the practice of Mr William Adams. William Norris was a founder of Norris and Miles, a solicitors' practice still housed in Market Square.

As a deeply religious man, he was a great servant to the Church of England. He lived at The Mount and worshipped regularly at St Mary's, Tenbury, and from 1872 he was the people's warden. He was also a regular Sunday School teacher 'where his earnest advice and pious example are not likely to be lost upon those to whom his instruction was imparted'.

Mr Norris's many unpaid offices in the Hereford Diocese included honorary secretary and treasurer of the Queen Victoria Clergy Fund, which assisted clergymen on low salaries; honorary lay secretary to the Hereford Diocesan Conference and to the Hereford Diocesan Finance Association.

*William Norris*

William Norris was a strong defender of the Church of England, speaking out against the advocates of disestablishment and disendowment. He believed that the best way to uphold the Church was by educating the young in the history and position of the Church in this country and countering the fallacious arguments of the Church's opponents. His role in the administration of Tenbury National (Church of England) School contributed greatly towards its success and ensured that it was not necessary to provide a secular School Board school when the 1870 Education Act was passed.

In planning the establishment of St Michael's College as a choir school, Sir Frederick Gore Ouseley, on discovering that the late Harriet Rushout of Burford House had left £600 in her will for building a church at Oldwood, set about forming a parish which the new church would serve. There was opposition to this, notably from the vicar of Tenbury, whose curate Ouseley had been. William Norris wrote to contradict the opinion of his own vicar saying: 'It is very painful to me to be acting in seeming opposition to the clergymen of my parish. I cannot understand the fact of Sir Frederick formerly having been a curate of Mr Bennett as sufficient reason for opposing the accomplishment of such a work. Ouseley is a good man whose principles our Bishop is willing to guarantee. It is the bounden duty of every right minded person in the parish to do his utmost to forward such a work. There are a number of families on the outskirts of the Tenbury Parish living in a state of practical heathenism.'

The opposition died away and the new church and college were built. Norris and Miles even acted as solicitors for the college.

*The Rev. Sir Frederick Gore Ouseley*

His interest also extended to the railways. The Tenbury Railway from Wooferton to Tenbury was opened in 1861, the Tenbury to Bewdley Railway in 1864. Each railway was run by a separate company and William Norris was solicitor to both until they were taken over by the Great Western Railway in 1870. William Norris took his duties seriously and fiercely contested the contractor's claim of £11,689 for additional costs for the Tenbury to Bewdley line.

Mr Norris was also one of the principal promoters of the Tenbury Corn Exchange, which opened in 1858. In honour of the occasion he was presented with a silver candelabra, drawing room clock and a gold watch and chain. The building on Teme Street, still known as the Corn Exchange, is now occupied by Bedford Dials.

A ploughing match was held to commemorate the opening of the Exchange and from this the Tenbury Agricultural Society was inaugurated. As might be expected, William Norris was the honorary secretary from then until a few years before his death. On his retirement from the post he was presented with a testimonial in appreciation of his valuable services to the Society.

William was also prominent in the formation of the Tenbury Company of the Worcestershire Volunteers (later to become part of the Territorial Army) in 1859, when the Tenbury Rifle Volunteer Company was formed. He first served as a lieutenant and was presented to Queen Victoria with the officers. When Captain Pardoe resigned from the command in 1871 he suggested that William should take over because of his knowledge of the working of the company and his devotion to drill. William however declined, saying that he thought the landed gentry should contribute. His suggestion was acted upon and Captain Bailey of Rosedale took over. When he retired in 1878 Lieutenant Norris replaced him and held the post until 1884 when war office regulations required him to relinquish it. He retired with the honorary rank of Major and was permitted to continue wearing the uniform of the Regiment. On his retirement he was presented with a silver inkstand bearing the figure of a volunteer and a silver claret jug and also received the Victoria Decoration for long service.

At the ceremony for cutting the first sod for the building of the Pump Room in 1861, Lieutenant Norris commanded the Volunteers who marched to the ground in full uniform led by their drum and fife band and with their new colours flying. According to a contemporary report: after the cutting of the first sod by Mrs Wheeler and the usual speeches, the Volunteers presented arms; the National Anthem was played and the church bells rang out, the Volunteers firing two volleys to conclude the ceremony. They then marched to Kyrewood House for a celebratory lunch provided by Mr Wheeler. Lieutenant Norris proposed the health of Mr Wheeler in eulogistic terms and also that of Mr G. Pardoe, the announcement of their both accepting office in the Volunteers being received with the most enthusiastic applause. The Volunteers then marched back to their depot and were dismissed after a short drill, expressing a wish that all their campaigns might be as pleasant.

William Norris held many other positions in and around Tenbury including: Clerk to the Tenbury County Court and the Magistrates of the Tenbury and Burford Divisions; Chairman of the Tenbury Parish Council; Secretary of the Tenbury Wells Hotel and Boarding Company; Secretary of the Tenbury Fishing Association, which he set up to encourage more people to stay in Tenbury and hence more visitors to the Pump Rooms; Member of the local Board of Health; Trustee of Philip Bailey's Charity; Honorary Secretary and Treasurer of the Tenbury Dispensary; Honorary member of Foresters Court; Relieving Officer for the District; and Member of the Local Lodge of Oddfellows.

William Norris's private life was not so successful as his public one and his first marriage ended in divorce – a rare and scandalous occurrence at the time.

He had married Miss Louisa Denikee, the daughter of a physician in 1847 – 'a young lady of great personal attractions and accomplishments'. For a while they lived happily but had no children. One can't help wondering whether William's many activities left his young wife feeling neglected. In 1854 the Rev. George Giles came to Tenbury as a curate and became a close friend of the Norrises, frequently visiting their home. When he had an attack of rheumatic fever in 1855, Mr Norris treated him with great kindness and attention.

In February 1857 the Norrises visited the Isle of Wight to give Mrs Norris a change of air. She remained there with a relative, Lady Holmes, while her husband returned to Tenbury. In March, Louisa left by coach for Cowes, saying that her husband had sent for her.

*Two views of The Mount, the home of William Norris*

Shortly before this George Giles left Tenbury and for a while nothing was heard of them. They were eventually traced by Mr Jones, William's attorney, to a house in Vauxhall Bridge Road, London, where they were living as man and wife under the name of Mr and Mrs Grant. It transpired that in the September before they had stayed under that name at Liddington's Hotel in Paternoster Row. These facts were proved in court by Rev. T. Norris, William's brother; Mr Sweet, a physician in Tenbury; Mr Jones and other witnesses when William sued for divorce.

The Divorce and Matrimonial Causes Act had only recently been passed and this was one of the first occasions (May 1858) that a case had been heard by the full court. Hearing the matter were the Lord Chief Justice Campbell, Lord Chief Baron Pollock and Sir C. Creswell, Judge Ordinary. Previously a divorce could only be obtained by having an Act of Parliament passed after an investigation before the House of Lords – a procedure not readily available to the man in the street. Dr Twiss and Mr W.H. Cooke represented William.

Louisa and George were in court but they had made no answer to the divorce petition. Their attorney, Mr Cole, was allowed to cross examine the witnesses but he was not allowed to make a statement on behalf of the defendants.

In the words of the Lord Chief Justice: 'You were summoned to appear in the Court and you were at liberty to put in an answer; but not having done so

*The offices of Norris & Miles, solicitors, in Market Square today*

and not having denied the allegations of the petition, you cannot now be heard on the case. It seems to us that a person has no right to be heard not having put in an answer; it would be most inconvenient if it were so. It may have the effect of changing the whole aspect of the case at the hearing, without giving any notice to the petitioner. In this case the petitioner is entitled to the remedy he prays, viz. a dissolution of the marriage. The marriage is proved and subsequent co-habitation, there is no ground for suspecting collusion and the adultery is clearly proved.'

Mr Cole applied to be heard on the question of costs but this was refused and costs were awarded to 'the paramour' George Giles. The court decided it had no power to vary the marriage settlement.

It is not known what happened to Louise and George. It must have been very much a love match between them as they faced strong social ostracism for their actions at the time. In 1859 William married Phoebe Nicholls of Shrewsbury, who strongly supported him for many years.

William died on 27 December 1904. Because of age and failing health he had reduced his public activities but continued to work as a solicitor. He left his office at 3:30 pm and went to his home at The Mount, where he died of heart failure an hour later.

His funeral at St Michael's Church was a grand affair. Business in Tenbury was largely suspended, shutters were closed, blinds drawn and the muffled church bells pealed. The Volunteers fittingly headed the cortege, followed by members of the Spring of Providence Lodge of Oddfellows, the Ancient Order of Foresters and the great and good of Tenbury.

The procession was met at the gates by the Rev. J. Hampton, Warden of St Michael's College, who read the opening sentences of the Burial Service. When all had taken their places in the church, the hymn, *Art thou weary, art thou languid?* was sung. The psalm *Lord, thou hast been our refuge* was read by the Rev. J.B. Joyce, alternate verses being taken up by the congregation. The Rev. W.N.G. Eliot, vicar of Tenbury, read the lesson. The hymn *Now the labourer's task is o'er* was rendered and then the funeral procession went to the place of interment at the east end of the church close to the grave of Sir Frederick Gore Ouseley. The Bishop of Hereford said the words of committal and also pronounced the blessing.

It was a fitting end for a great servant of Tenbury.

# Tenbury Fire Brigade

The first fire station in Tenbury, subsequently a mortuary, still stands outside the entrance to St Mary's Church on Church Street. Much of the information that follows comes from R.A. Hartland (whose family were members of the early brigade), with some additional points from Howard Miller.

The Church Street fire station was erected in 1858. This was a substantial single storey brick building, with slated roof, having only the one room used as the Appliance Room. This was fronted by a pair of heavy doors, arched at the top, similar to the church doors. In the one door a window was situated to give light, in the other was a very small pane of glass which could be smashed to give access to the door key. The building became a mortuary when vacated by the Fire Brigade in 1936 and still stands at the gates to St Mary's church.

*The old fire station building outside the entrance to St Mary's church.*
*The double doors still show evidence of the window which provided some*
*natural light, and the smaller one which could be smashed to provide*
*access to the door key*

The first appliances have not been recorded, but by 1874 the Brigade had received a new machine, as reported in the *Tenbury Advertiser* for 9 June 1874:

> The engine is what is called a London Brigade Fire Engine and is procured from Messrs Shand, Mason & Co. It is to be worked by twenty-two men, and is provided with three 40 foot lengths of hose, two 6 foot lengths of suction hose, canvas and leather buckets. A small portable hand engine has also been purchased and will be found useful for getting at a fire in the attic.

### Rules and Regulations of The Tenbury Fire Brigade 1887

1) The Brigade shall be called the Tenbury Fire Brigade and shall consist of a Captain, Dep Captain and not less than 10 firemen under the general control of the Lighting Inspectors of Tenbury Town.

2) The appointment of Captain and Dep Captain shall be in the hands of the Lighting Inspectors who shall also have the power of appointing and dismissing the Firemen.

3) The Captain shall take command of the Brigade. He shall endeavour to ascertain the cause of fires, also whether the buildings were insured and in what office. He shall report regularly to the Lighting Inspectors at their meetings. He shall visit the Engine House at least once in each week. He shall keep a book to enter and account of work done and all transactions connected with the Brigade.

4) The Dep Captain shall perform the duties of Captain, in his absence, whether from ill health or other cause.

5) The Captain shall be paid the sum of £3 and the Dep Captain £1 yearly. For each fire the Captain shall be paid 3s for the first hour at a fire and 1s 6d for each succeeding hour and the Dep Captain 2s 6d for the first hour and 1s 3d for each succeeding hour.

   An allowance of £1 a year shall be made to the caretaker, who shall be appointed by the Inspectors.

   The firemen shall receive 5s each yearly and for attendance at each practise 1s. For every time they are employed at a fire 2s for the first hour and 1s for each succeeding hour either night or day.

This second appliance '… was a hand-drawn hose-cart fitted with solid rubber tyred wheels. This carried eight lengths of canvas hose, standpipes, keys and two branches and a dividing breeching, as well as two oil lamps, fixed to the front. With this hose-cart a fire could be tackled quickly using water under pressure from the water mains. In addition, the Brigade possessed a hand-pump – a metal bucket like container with a hand-pump fixed in the centre – with a short length of small bore canvas hose attached with nozzle, the whole pump transported by means of a brass rail affixed around the top. The reservoir was filled with the canvas buckets provided from a suitable water supply. This pump was useful for small fires, such as timber under hearths, etc.

The fireman's uniform was the usual blue melton double-breasted fire tunic and trousers, the latter with thin red stripes down the outside seams, except for the Captain who had black braid on his trousers and also black interwoven cord on his tunic cuffs. All wore leather belts and pouches carrying wooden handled axes. Some firemen carried hose or nozzle spanners and belt lines. The Captain and Deputy carried whistles on chains.

The helmets worn by the Captain and Deputy were the standard brass helmet with the standard badge, crossed axes with torch. The firemen wore black leather helmets with a brass rim fitted all around the peak and neck piece, two brass rosettes, one each side at the top of the leather chin strap, with a brass chain over the front of the peak between the rosettes. The letters TFB in brass were placed on the front of the helmet, and a small brass number between 1 and 10. Calf length leather fire boots were worn.

A month's notice of dismissal, or of retirement from the Brigade, had to be given.

---

**Scale of Charges for Attending Fires** [undated]
(per day of 10 hours or any part thereof)

For the use of the Engine and service of the Brigade within a distance of 6 miles from the Engine House

| | £ s d | | £ s d |
|---|---|---|---|
| Engine | 2 2 0 | Deputy-Captain, 1st hour | 3 6 |
| Horses | 2 2 0 | Ditto, each subsequent hour | 1 0 |
| Captain | 1 1 0 | Firemen, 1st hour | 3 0 |
| Driver | 5 0 | Ditto, each subsequent hour | 1 0 |
| Ditto at night | 7 6 | Assistant engaged for each hour | 1 0 |
| Captain, 1st hour | 7 0 | | |
| Ditto, each subsequent hour | 3 0 | Refreshments, at actual cost | |

A further charge will be made where the distance or time exceed the above limits.

## Nov 14th 1906 Fire at Harp Bank, Burford

At 6:30 p.m. T. Lambert informed me that Mrs Williams, Harp Bank, Burford required the assistance of the fire brigade, her house being on fire. He had ordered the horses from the Swan Hotel on his way to give the alarm.

The brigade was called out and mustered quickly and were waiting for horses some time.

The fireman was again sent and orders given to drag the engine. The horses were met in Teme Street by the Corn Exchange, proceeding to the station very quietly and without a responsible driver.

The engine was horsed with difficulty owing to the collar on one horse being larger than the brigade harness would fit. A belt had to be used.

Arrived at the fire at 6:53. Found the staircase badly burnt. One bedroom floor, three doors and the roof charred. One bedroom and various boxes burnt.

A lingering fire kept breaking out in the roof timbers.

It is surprising how the few people there were, with the short supply of water, had managed to keep the fire under, and that the whole building had not been gutted.

The hand pump was used which soon got blocked and useless through the filthy liquid sent through it.

I should say the cause was from a match or candle being used under or near the stairs and quite accidental.

The building is not insured and belongs to Mrs Williams.

I estimate the loss at £20 – 0 – 0.

The following were engaged:

| | | |
|---|---|---|
| Capt R.W. Jarvis | 3½ hours | £1-10-6 |
| Dept Capt S. Dadge | 3½ hours | 7-3 |
| Fmn W. Hartland | 4 hours | 6-0 |
| Fmn J. Allen | 3½ hours | 5-6 |
| " J. Turford | 2½ hours | 4-6 |
| " R. Palmer | 2½ hours | 4-6 |
| " S. Ward | 4 hours | 6-0 |
| " J. Taylor | 2½ hours | 4-6 |
| " E. Mills | 2½ hours | 4-6 |
| " T. Wakeman | 2½ hours | 4-6 |
| " H. Turner | 2½ hours | 4-6 |
| Helper T. Lambert | 3 hours | 3-0 |
| Cleaning | | 5-0 |
| Engine, etc | | 2-2-0 |
| Two horses | | 2-2-0 |
| Driver Hancocks | | 5-0 |
| | | 8-19-3 |

Sent to Mrs Williams Nov 21st 1906 and paid Feb 16th 1907

*Copy of a fire report by R.W. Jarvis, Capt. Tenbury Fire Brigade*

*Parade for the fire crew, engine and management committee, c.1910*

The horsing of the manual engine was usually by standing arrangement with the Swan Hotel, Burford. The Swan Hotel had a number of horses in their stables to cater for their coaches, and an alarm bell was fitted to their stables. There was also one in the Coachman's cottage nearby for night calls. In the

*Mrs Wheeler starts the new engine in 1913*

*The fire crew dealing with a fire at Kyrewood on 24 September 1914*

event of a fire, a pair of horses could be quickly galloped up Teme Street, Market Street and into Church Street to be harnessed up.

The call out system was by electric bell in the firemen's houses. This was operated by the local Police, and maintained by the General Post Office. However, in the event of a failure of the bells, all firemen in Tenbury had an

*An exercise in manhandling the fire engine*

enamelled metal plate over their doorway inscribed 'Fireman'. An enamelled plate still remains on the Fireman's Cottage in Berrington Road.

The usual complement of the Brigade consisted of twelve men: the Officer in Charge, his Deputy and ten firemen.

Sadly and ironically, early historical records of the Fire Brigade were lost in a fire at the Council Boardroom, Teme Street in the late 1920s. However, some snippets are known, largely from the Gas Inspectors Minute Book, 1877-1895 (perhaps recorded here because the fire brigade was under the general control of the Lighting Inspectors of Tenbury, also responsible for the gas street lighting). On 15 July 1887, the fire engine was tested at the entrance to the River Teme by the bridge. It was found to be in thoroughly good working order. However the length of pipe at 160 feet was noted to be much shorter than that at Burford, where 600 feet was available. On 24 April 1889 it was recorded that Mr Hardemann of the Swan kept the horses for the Fire Engine. In 1912 a

---

As announced in our issue of last week, Mr. Samuel Dadge passed away in his 78th year on Thursday, July 24th, at 80 Droitwich Road, Worcester.

The deceased had only left Tenbury some two months ago to enjoy his retirement in Worcester. As a parting gift from his Tenbury friends, he took with him a handsome chair, and it was hoped he would live many years to enjoy its use. This, however, was not to be.

The Vicar of Tenbury (Rev. J.A. Chesterton) referring to Mr. Dadge in his sermon on Sunday morning, said: 'He was an example to all of us, of simple and very beautiful faith, expressing itself in loyal service and devotion. For over 40 years he had been Parish Clerk here, friend of everybody, respected by all, and now he has passed on. Our thoughts and prayers are with him.'

The deceased during his long residence in the town as a master farrier had been a member of the Tenbury Fire Brigade for upwards of 40 years, having gained the long service medal and retiring with the position of Deputy captain.

As a member of the Ancient Order of Oddfellows at Bewdley, he shared in the sorrows and joys of the 'Spring of Providence' Lodge, Tenbury.

The coffin, which was of polished Oak with heavy brass furniture, bore the inscription:

SAMUEL DADGE
At Rest,
July 24th, 1930
Aged 78 years.

---

*Newspaper clipping 1930, (unattributed)*

secondhand Mason steamer was purchased for £345 capable of pumping 200 gallons of water per minute.

---

Saturday, Nov 6th 1910
Fire at Eastham Grange
5 miles from Tenbury

At 4:30 p.m. alarm was received and upon arriving at the Fire Station, the Brigade were informed that a large fire was raging at Eastham Grange.

There was a slight delay in getting horses through, only one man being at the stables. A messenger was despatched to enquire cause and with his assistance, the Engine was quickly horsed, the leader ridden by Fireman W. Hartland, Jr.

It was very dark and the weather extremely bad, a violent snowstorm raging, which completely obscured the roadway and made it most difficult to drive distances, the horses who were unable to travel rapidly getting continually balled with snow and making the journey most dangerous.

Upon arrival at the fire, found the farm buildings forming three sides of a square in flames. Water was most difficult to get although plentiful. Pipers Brook running in a deep ravine close by. The Engine had to be taken back into the roadway and got down to the watercourse the opposite side of the stream where 30' of suction was required and 750' of delivery hose used. The water was immediately directed to the building almost adjoining the house, and with great difficulty, fire there extinguished.

Owing to the scarcity of helpers, instead of having 25 to 30 pumpers, only such members of the Brigade who were not laying hose with the assistance of Inspector Lane, a man and a boy, were available at the pump and it was surprising they were able to pump water up such a precipitous place and onto the fire.

A steam engine was greatly needed.

Before the fire was safely extinguished I was informed the pumpers were exhausted, but I begged of them to continue for a short time.

About 6:00 a.m. a few helpers began to arrive and better progress was made, and after pulling down dangerous gables the Brigade was able to leave, arriving at the Fire Station at 1:00 p.m.

The damage done was very extensive, a three stall stable and a two box hacking stable, coach house, four stall cart horse stable, harness rooms and cleaning rooms with lofts and Grooms' rooms over.

Large three bay barn, including a quantity of implements, three hop kilns and cooling rooms, shed, cowhouse, granary were burnt out, only the walls being left.

*A fire report of the time*

Subsequent information can be gleaned from the *Tenbury Wells Advertiser* as follows:

14 November 1936: 'A report was read from the Burford and Tenbury Fire Brigade Committee in which the tenancy of the new fire station was accepted at a rental of £30 per year. Nov 28th was fixed for the official opening.'

5 December 1936: 'On Sat. evening, Nov 28th, a complimentary dinner was given to members of the Tenbury Fire Brigade at the Bridge Hotel, by members of the Fire Brigade Committee on the occasion of the Fire Engine being transferred to its new home.' (The first fire attended from the new station was one at Woofferton Saw Mills.)

16 October 1937: 'Tenbury RDC recommended to buy a Leyland motor fire engine after trials of three engines. The trials were held in a field opposite the Tenbury Hospital and included a trial run to the Fox at Broadheath.'

30 April 1938: 'On Sat. next May 7th the public will have the opportunity of seeing Tenbury Fire Brigade's new engine. Mrs Rollo has consented to start up the engine after which a demonstration will be given at The Burgage at 6:00 p.m.'

7 May 1938: 'Tenbury's new Fire Engine is one of the lighter type Leyland Fire Fighting models. It is powered by a 6 cylinder which develops 85 bhp.

*Tenbury Fire Brigade in the late 1960s.*
*Back row: Ron Beavan, Simon Sadler, Geoff Bristow, John Bradley*
*and Roy Tompkins*
*Front row: Len James, Bob Capp, 'Golly' Gibbons (Captain), Don James*
*and John James*

The pumping unit is located at the rear of the machine and is of the two stage turbine pump, capable of pumping 500/700 gallons of water per minute. A 40 gallon first aid tank is fitted to the machine so that water can be directed on a fire before the main pump is coupled to the water mains. The type of body is known as the New World body. The equipment includes brackets for the Brigade's existing escape, four 8 ft lengths of suction house and Trakgrip tyres.'

The new Leyland had been delivered on 25 April 1938 and its first fire was at the Hop Pickers Barracks by The Talbot, Newnham Bridge on 15 August 1938.

In 1941 the National Fire Service was formed and the Tenbury Fire Brigade became part of it. This arrangement continued until after the war when Tenbury became part of the Worcester City and County Fire Brigade. In 1974, with local government reorganisation, the Hereford & Worcester Fire Brigade took over Tenbury's requirements. Then when the county was again divided into Hereford and Worcester, fire protection remained a joint county operation.

Today Tenbury is served by a two appliance retained station that is actually sited in Shropshire.

# The Tenbury Races

A racecourse on Oldwood Common – about a mile out of Tenbury – was known as 'one of the oldest and best racecourses in England'. It was a busy place when horse racing was popular during the 18th and 19th centuries.

An advertisement for Tenbury Races at the New Course at Old Wood appears in the *Gloucester Journal* in 1736, which suggests that this may have been one of the first meetings to be held there. Three years later, in 1739, the *Worcester Postman* (later *Berrows Worcester Journal*) contained the following advertisement:

> On Wednesday 18th July next will be run for on the Old Wood course near Tenbury, a saddle, bridle and whip value two guineas, the best of three four mile heats, to pay one shilling and six pence entrance or five shillings at the post. The best horse if required to be sold for ten guineas to any subscriber.
>
> On Thursday 19th ... a purse of ten guineas by hunters that have never won the value of £20 in plate or money, to carry eleven stone, saddle and bridle included ...
>
> On Friday 20th ... a purse of five guineas by ponies 13 hands high, to carry eight stone, saddle and bridle included ...
>
> No less than three horses shall start for either of the paid purses and no less than two for the saddle, bridle and bit. Every horse to be entered at the Market House in Tenbury for the said purses six days before the day of running ...
>
> NB There will be cock fighting every morning.

Tenbury did not attract the attention of the Racing Calendar until 1792. For a long period all races at Old Wood were flat and designed for the lower grades of runners and riders. The race meeting was financed by subscribers, local people who put up the money for prizes. Only subscribers were permitted to shoe the participating horses, stable them overnight and provide booths for the sale of food and drink. A local dignitary was elected as Steward to oversee the organisation.

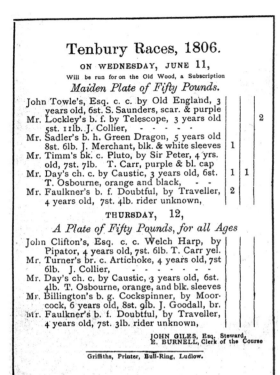

*A race card from 1806*

The race meetings were great social events, attracting every level of society, with plenty of side shows and refreshments available. The Steward provided an ordinary (slap up meal) at the Town Hall whilst a Ball was held in the evening. There was possibly a theatre in Tenbury in 1813, as the Worcester Company performed every evening of race week.

By 15 March 1860, steeplechasing had been introduced, when *Berrows Worcester Journal* reported, 'This was entirely an amateur affair, got up without the least assistance from professionals, and proved on the whole successful … The weather was most propitious and the

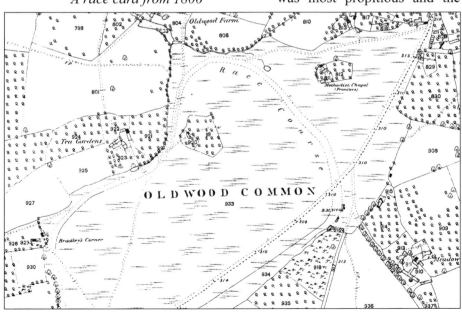

*An OS Map of Oldwood Common from 1884 showing most of the racecourse*

company, if not quite as numerous as at the summer meeting, was certainly more respectable.'

In the 1860s a pattern seems to have been developed of a spring meeting for steeplechasing and a summer meeting for the flat. By this time races also took place near The Swan Hotel in Burford.

On 17 March 1864 a meeting was held in the large field near The Swan with a detour along meadows adjoining the new railway line to Tudors Field then into the straight bounded by the Worcester to Ludlow road. (The Tenbury to Bewdley railway opened in 1864.) At this meeting the Maiden Plate steeplechase of 2 sovereigns with 15 added was for horses 'that had never won a steeplechase and had fairly hunted with the Ludlow, Worcestershire and Hereford hounds'. It was a dramatic affair. Captain Brown's *Deodora* refused the first fence, unseated her rider at the third and fell at the first fence of the second lap. Mr Mytton's *Maid of All Work* also unseated her rider on the second lap, but he remounted to win.

The meeting on 9 May 1877 comprised seven races – two steeplechases, three over hurdles and two on the flat. Opposite the grandstand were the paddock, weighing and dressing tents. The punters were well looked after too – there were tents for refreshments, shooting galleries, merry-go-rounds and shows. The special return train from Bewdley induced many to come who otherwise would have had to stay overnight in Tenbury. The *Tenbury Wells Advertiser* reported that 'vast crowds of people wended their way to the race course from all quarters'.

On 22 April 1879 the ground set aside for licensed victuallers was let by auction. Mr Mattock of Royal Oak paid £7 for the land next to the paddock, whilst Mr Hall of the Wine Vaults took the next lot for £3. These were the only Tenbury victuallers who took lots.

They might have regretted their bids, for between 1880 and 1886 there were no races because of an agricultural depression, but the revival of the meeting on 6 May 1887 was a great success. Some 800 to 900 people 'including many members of the light fingered fraternity' came by train from Birmingham.

The 1890 and 1900 meetings were at The Swan, possibly as it was more convenient for the railway. But then attendance began to decline. On 25 April 1904 there were many entries but not many horses actually ran, only 8 of the 17 entries ran in the Burford Selling Hurdle Race, and only 2 out of 8 in the Temeside Steeplechase. This was one of the last races held in the Tenbury area. Possibly the Ludlow meetings were more prestigious.

Now no sign remains of the courses at either Old Wood or The Swan. Grandstand Cottage at Old Wood, where the upper floor was originally tiered for seating the more important spectators, is now a private house. Booth Cottage nearby was used for selling drink and was appurtenanced to the Ship Inn in

**PRELIMINARY.**

# TENBURY RACES

### (ONE OF THE OLDEST ESTABLISHED MEETINGS IN ENGLAND),

Will be held on the

## OLD WOOD RACE COURSE,

ON

## FRIDAY, JULY 5th, 1889.

This Course is One Mile from the Town of Tenbury.

All information will be advertised in due course.

S. MATTOCK,

Secretary.

Royal Oak Hotel, Tenbury.

*A race poster from 1889*

Tenbury. It was sold to Sir Frederick Gore Ouseley as a school for children and then it too became a private house.

Oldwood Common, as it came to be known, was used to a limited extent for golf but by 1939 it was largely covered in bracken. In 1942 it was cleared for use in food production, with drainage dug by Italian prisoners of war. After the war it was grassed over and used for grazing sheep, but this had to cease as animals were being killed by the traffic. Now it is a favourite area for walking dogs.

# Accidents

Peaceful as it is, the area of Tenbury has not been without incidents of tragedy and triumph.

In January 1814 the Cambridge Coach was upset in a snowdrift. After 8 hours it was dragged out by the efforts of 14 carthorses but the occupants were almost frozen to death.

Along the side of the River Teme just outside the town, a footpath rises to the top of a cliff and was the scene of a tragic accident. The *Tenbury Wells Advertiser* for 12 September 1893 quotes from 'A Lover of the Picturesque and Beautiful' of 1846:

> It is remembered, when the rails were first erected, the footpath was truly perilous.
>
> In fact a dreadful accident once occurred, for want of such a fence; as a poor woman, who dwelt in that cottage, placed so snugly beneath the Cliff, was journeying home on a dark winter's night; not sufficiently regardful of her position, missed her footing – a scream was heard – there was a moment of fearful struggle, and the boiling flood passed over her!
>
> Poor Dorothea, thus was lost, but her name attached to the rock remains a sad memento, that she ever existed.

Thus was Dorothy's Rock so named.

Under the heading 'A Frightful Accident', the *Tenbury Wells Advertiser* for September 1880 reported the following:

> A frightful accident occurred on Saturday afternoon to a number of workmen who were returning from Clee Hill after leaving work on three trolleys down the steep incline of the railway. The line is about five miles long and branches off near the Ludlow railway station to the side of Titterstone Hill, which is situate at an altitude of 1730 feet above sea level. In descending the incline the utmost caution has to be used.

*Dorothy's Rock, scene of an accident in 1846*

It has been the custom for a long time for the workmen to mount a trolley on the top of the incline and ride on to Ludlow. The speed attained at some points of this dangerous journey may be imagined when the whole journey of nearly five miles is frequently accomplished in seven minutes. At some parts a mile a minute must have been reached ...

... There were brakes on the trolleys: 'a piece of wood which we press against the rim of the wheel.' The trolleys were connected with straps, and two planks, on which some of the men stood.

The number of workmen was about 40 on three trolleys, when ... a trolley conveying about 12 men suddenly left the metals, shooting the whole of the men, with one exception with terrible force upon the metal of the line. The exception was William Tranter of Hereford, who was pitched over a hedge into an adjoining field, and strange to say alighted on his legs without injury.

The other men presented a sad spectacle, the ground being covered with the bleeding and groaning. It was at first thought that several of them had been killed on the spot. The other men managed to stop their trolleys, and came to the rescue of their unfortunate comrades.

Two men died as a result of their injuries.

An agricultural fatality was reported in the *Tenbury Wells Advertiser* for 13 August 1889:

On Thursday morning Mr H.T. Weyman (district coroner) held an inquest at the Swan Hotel, Tenbury, on the body of John Robinson, aged 54, a labourer, employed on the Eardiston estate, who, as stated in our last issue, met with dreadful injuries through falling into some liquid which he was preparing for washing hop-poles. He was taken to the Cottage Hospital where he lingered until Tuesday, when he died. John Blunt said: I work for Mr Wallace and knew [the] deceased; on the 5th August we were going to get the stuff out of the tank to wash the poles; it was scalding hot; deceased got hold of the drag to pull the things back, and he slipped and fell in; I got him out as soon as I could; he was in about a minute and when I got him out I called Thomas Hill; he was sober; there was no larking or squabbling; I sent a conveyance with him to the hospital. … The jury returned a verdict of 'Accidental death'.

With increasing traffic on the roads it is to be expected that the papers soon started to carry news of motoring accidents, such as one that occurred on Polling Day, 19 January, in the General Election of 1906. Several electors were being taken to a polling station at Witley in a car belonging to Mr G. Hide of Shelsley Bank. The car skidded and fell about 9 feet down a bank into an adjoining field, ending up on its side. Whilst the car was wrecked, the occupants escaped with relatively minor injuries. Samuel Field had a fractured thigh and was taken to Tenbury Infirmary. Another had a rib broken and a third escaped with a broken wrist. Two of the occupants, William Field and James Hill, lived at Orleton. The newspaper notes that a committee was formed to help provide for the needs of the injured.

A sorry tale of a domestic accident was covered by the *Tenbury Wells Advertiser* on 26 December 1936:

Dorothy Mary Grace Jones aged 11 lived at Cleeton St Mary's, S. Shropshire. The child had no mother and helped her father with the housework in their cottage and looked after 2 younger children aged 5 and 2½. On Oct 1st while cleaning the hearth, her pinafore caught fire. Badly burned she removed some of her clothing, changed her frock and then walked ½ mile to a neighbour's house, carrying the baby with her. She collapsed at the neighbour's house and was taken to hospital where she died from exhaustion and toxaemia. The Coroner paid tribute to her fortitude and presence of mind in taking the baby with her.

A happier outcome was described in a report of 19 July 1941. On the 2nd of the month, at 4:50 p.m., Doreen Hughes, aged 10 of Wood Pit Cottage, Rochford was bathing in the River Teme. She was using an inflated rubber tube as a support but nevertheless ran into difficulties. Gwendoline Marshall, aged 13, a Girl Guide of Band Cottage, Rochford swam and supported her until a

Mr Martin, a soldier on 48 hours leave, and also of Band Cottage, arrived to complete the rescue. On Wednesday, 8 October, Gwendoline was presented with a parchment from the Royal Humane Society; an award also made to the serviceman.

The 1940s were a time for 'accidents' of another type, of course. In 1941 a Junkers 88 raider crashed into a wood on Brown Clee Hill. It hit the hillside with such force that bits of it were scattered over a wide area, but its bombs did not explode even though it burst into flames. The plane was seen to crash by the Home Guard who patrolled the area until all the crew of the bomber were accounted for, four members of which were later found dead near the plane. None had used a parachute.

A plaque has been placed on the Brown Clee near Abdon Buff to commemorate all those killed in plane crashes on the Clee Hills.

# Tenbury Hospital

Probably the best loved jewel in Tenbury is its tiny hospital. It is unique for many reasons but perhaps the most amazing is that it is there at all.

Park Villa was built in 1835 in Burford in a field on the side of the River Teme. It was a modest house owned by Richard Titt, a waiter at, and the eventual owner of, the Swan Hotel – a well known coaching stop on the route through Tenbury to London, North Wales and the ferry to Ireland. When he died in 1838 the house and land were left in a complicated legacy and with several mortgages, so it was some time before it came onto the market.

It was eventually purchased by Mrs Arabella Prescott for £2,678 and in 1871 she let it, rent-free, for one year to a committee of local well-known people who had been appointed to run it as St Mary's Cottage Hospital. At the end of that year, when the Annual Report was presented to the Committee, Mrs Prescott as President said that the hospital had proved its usefulness in the neighbourhood. An appeal was made to the public in and around Tenbury to support it by subscriptions.

Mrs Prescott, who had already given the house, garden, furniture and equipment free for one year, agreed to pay another quarter's expenses. However she would not take on the responsibility of engaging another nurse in place of the one in post, as she had just given in her notice. Nor would Mrs Prescott undertake the management of the hospital for another year. The Committee thus knew what it faced.

*Mrs Arabella Prescott*

109

The hospital was staffed by a nurse and servant, but records show that patients were required to help with some duties where possible. The local doctors gave their services free and the nurse-in-charge was, according to a report in the minute books of management committee, 'everything to be desired'.

A year later in 1872, the Committee Report says that 'most of those treated were industrious farm labourers, but only 12 farmers were subscribers'. Mrs Prescott offered the whole premises for sale; the asking price was £2,000, but Lord Northwick, who was interested in buying it, was willing to offer only £1,750. After what must have been a few difficult months, Lord Northwick's offer was accepted. It was then leased to the Committee at a rate of 1s per year for a period of 10 years. Rules were adopted, a management committee appointed and subscriptions solicited. The nurse was paid £7 10s and the servant £2 10s per quarter.

Throughout the following years additions to the provision were made and extensions built onto the original house, among them the veranda – possibly for the open-air treatment of patients suffering from tuberculosis, which was common at the time.

The years 1890-1894 were not happy ones as there seem to have been staffing problems, but they were resolved and in 1897, as a tribute to Queen Victoria in her Golden Jubilee year, it was decided that the town should buy the hospital. This cost was a reasonable £340 and subscriptions were raised.

*The façade of the hospital in 1907*

Later, when Lady Northwick read that the Committee would have to withdraw capital to pay some of the running expenses she gave £100 to pay the debt.

From that time the hospital continued to develop and in 1912 the Elizabeth Wing was added to the side of the original house. *The Nursing Mirror* noted it as 'having 4 airy wards, 10 beds and 2 bathrooms and being very fit for its purpose'. Sadly, however, staffing difficulties and rising costs led to the closure of the hospital in 1928.

At a Public Meeting in 1930 the *Tenbury Wells Advertiser* noted that there were some differing opinions following a proposal made earlier by Tenbury Parish Council that the hospital remain closed. Someone asked, 'What would the Founder think?' The vicar thought that its day had passed and others thought that it might not be missed by the subscribers, but would be missed by the poorer people of the district.

At a meeting in November of the same year, attended by representatives from 17 local parishes, there was strong support for the motion that it should be renamed 'The Tenbury and District Hospital and Nursing Association'. The object was to provide complete medical services, treatment at home by district nurses and at Tenbury District Hospital, Kidderminster, Worcester or Birmingham hospitals when necessary.

The Prescott family tradition of support for the hospital was continued by Colonel W.R. Prescott, a great-grandson of Mrs Arabella Prescott. He was Chairman of the Committee that worked for the re-opening of the hospital, and remained Chairman until he was recalled to the Army in 1939. As a result of all the district support and public meetings, the hospital was re-opened on 3 September 1931 by the Archdeacon of Ludlow.

The nursing staff consisted of a Sister, Miss Proctor, a staff nurse and two Queen's nurses for the district. A subscription scheme of 4d per week per household was started. This was collected by voluntary helpers who visited anyone wishing to contribute, which helped to fund the upkeep. The original Management Committee consisted of the vicar of Tenbury, the Rev. Ayscough-Smith as Chairman, together with Rev. J.W. Joyce, Rev. W. Miles, R. Prescott-Decie, T. Grove, W. Norris, G. Pardoe, F.W. Preston, E.V. Wheeler, Dr Murray, J.L. Sweet, W. Powell, W. Taylor, Rev. McLoughlin and W.E. Tait.

Fundraising has continued ever since; a need for extra cash would arise and from somewhere it arrived. Mrs W.S. Davis paid for two extra bedrooms and 'conveniences'. In 1934/5 another extension was built, beyond the Elizabeth Wing, by W. Hewitt, the town's main builder of the time, who lived at Cornwall House in Cross Street. The cost was £3,157 10s 0d, which funded an equipped operating theatre, a men's ward and a women's ward.

*An aerial view of the hospital c.2002*

In addition new gates were erected and a driveway was built. All except the wards were funded by Mr Malcolm Rollo of Rochford House in memory of his parents.

Radio was put into the wards in 1937 and an ambulance was given by Messrs Bedford and Merritt. For several years, even after the NHS had taken it over, it was housed at Mr G. Maund's garage in Teme Street and often driven either by him or by one of his staff. Special volunteer night drivers were trained in elementary first aid and according to anecdotal history, also in certain driving techniques!

Penlu, the house next door, was bought by Dr Blundell-Williams in 1943 and, as he did not wish to live there, he offered the lease of it at an annual rent of £75, with the option of buying it in the future. In 1944 it was occupied as a nurses' home and now it is owned by the Tenbury Sports Club who rent it out three times a week to Age Concern.

Slowly but surely the hospital was growing and becoming a very useful and well used part of community life.

When the National Heath Service (NHS) came into being on 5 July 1948 it did not spell the end of the district's commitment to keeping Tenbury and district's hospital in the best possible order. Supported by representatives of seven parishes, the League of Friends of Tenbury Hospital came into being.

The Friends quickly realised that funds would be needed to keep it functioning and appropriate for the rest of the 20th century and beyond. In the early days, the responsibilities of the Friends were not onerous:

visiting patients, organising daily papers, arranging for and funding patient convalescence – but this soon developed into provision of a huge range of amenities for patients and staff.

Some of the Friends' splendid achievements include:

1954 Improvements made to the operating theatre.

1956 A building fund created to improve outpatients department.

1971 This year was the centenary of the founding of the hospital and a Centenary Fund Committee was established to raise funds to buy land east of the hospital for a car park. This effort was so successful that there were sufficient extra funds to provide piped oxygen and suction to wards, and gas for the operating theatre.

1981 £20,000 was given towards the X-ray department.

1986 An outpatients department was built on land belonging to the Friends and leased to the Hospital Trust.

1992 The operating theatre was re-built with its own recovery ward and up to date ventilation system.

Recently porches have been built over the outer doors to give cover to patients arriving by car or ambulance.

Also £160,000 has been given towards the £335,000 cost of upgrading the operating theatre and providing a new sanitary annexe between the two main wards.

2000 A Millennium Project was completed in two phases: an extension containing a day case unit; en-suite single bed palliative care unit with courtyard garden; consulting room; community nursing staff offices and store room; a physiotherapy unit with office; occupational therapy room with kitchen for patients' rehabilitation; podiatry and audiology rooms; reception and waiting area with children's section and toilets for the disabled.

When completed, this new block was leased to the NHS Trust, which now manages the hospital after the most recent NHS reforms and which had contributed £80,000. Further contributions were made by the Eveson Trust and the Jordan Foundation, but the local community had provided in one way or another the remaining £670,000.

With this kind of heritage it is not surprising that whenever the opportunity arises, the hospital and its Friends can still count on the enthusiastic support of the people of Tenbury and district. After all, it is one of the jewels of the town.

The Tenbury Hospital is, however, not the only institution to have provided care for Tenbury. In 1871 a fever hospital was erected in the grounds of the

Tenbury Union Workhouse. Lord Northwick of Tenbury provided £828, three-quarters of the cost, in celebration of his marriage. It served the workhouse until both were closed in 1932. It then became the offices of Russell, Baldwin and Bright until sold again in 2005.

In addition to the fever hospital, an isolation hospital was built about 1890 on the same site in a timber-framed building given by Francesca Baldwyn-Childe of Kyre Park. It was for the treatment of hop-pickers who came to the area with infectious diseases. It also closed with the workhouse in 1932 and has now been demolished.

# Meadows Mill

> Perhaps when you've used up your North Sea oil
> And your fossil fuel is done,
> You'll remember I once was a watermill,
> And that rivers will always run.
>
> 'The Song of the Watermill' in *Down along Temeside* by Richard Holdings, 1979

For thousands of years the people of Tenbury Wells and district have exploited the benefit of waterpower. Before the coming of coal driven steam power, the water mill was often the centre of the local economy. This fact did not escape the notice of William the Conqueror's surveyors in 1086 when compiling the tax record known as the Domesday Book. Several local parishes are quoted as having a water mill, but the description of one seems very like Meadows Mill in Eardiston.

> In the Doddingtree Hundred - St Mary's holds EARDISTON and 8 ploughs: KNIGHTON (on Teme) for the Monks' supplies. The two manors are of 15 hides ... In lordship 8 ploughs: A priest, 15 villagers and 10 smallholders with 15 ploughs; A further 3 ploughs would be possible. 17 slaves. A mill at 10s; a fishery; meadow, 6 acres; woodland half a league long and 3 furlongs wide. Value £8

Perhaps the mill was established by Eardwulf, a Saxon whose name evolved to become Eardiston, first referred to in a Saxon chronicle as Eardulfeston (*c*.957 'the farm of Eardwulf').

In records prepared in 1240 by the monks of St Mary's Priory, Worcester, Meadows Mill is referred to as *mol de Medewye* (on the way to the 'mead' or 'meadow'). It records that the annual rental to be paid to the priory was six marks per year.

The miller was not always the most popular person in the community. Although usually a tenant, he could gain an extra benefit by not declaring the true yield of a load of grain, either to his landlord or to his customer, and keeping the extra for himself. The word emoluments, used in a company's financial accounts

*Berrington Mill, west of Tenbury on Cadmore Brook*

to state the amount of directors' fees/wages i.e. a sum they have kept for themselves after paying all other expenses, is from the Latin *emolumentum*, the fee paid to the miller. *Molere* is Latin for grind.

Milling was a highly skilled trade often passed down from father to son. One such family was the Moores, who were millers in the Teme valley for many generations. The earliest positive record of the Moore family as millers was obtained from a journal in the possession of a descendant now living in the United States. This describes a Thomas Moore who was a miller at Meadows Mill in the first half of the 18th century. Three generations of Thomas Moores lived in Meadows Mill from at least 1794, where the journal's author and his father were born. The author's grandfather, however, was born in 1761 at Butterworth Mill, Eastham (location unknown), and prior to becoming the miller at Meadows Mill he milled at Creeks Mill, Hanley Childe, and Stockton Mill, where some of his many children were born. Moore family christenings and burials are

*Meadows Mill in the 1900s with eel trap (left) and mill wheel but after the building had been converted to a summer house by the Wallaces*

recorded in the parish records of Lindridge, Eastham and Hanley William. According to these records, other members of the same Moore family were also millers at Hanley Mill for at least a couple of generations until 1834, when the wife of John Moore died at the age of only 39. However, the author himself probably never became a miller, first moving to Birmingham to become a jeweller working for a Mr Matthews and finally emigrating to the United States in 1873.

By 1841, according to the first census to contain names, Edward Foley was the miller, and in the 1851 census he and his wife employed four other living-in workers/servants, so the mill was probably still quite prosperous. It is not known why the Moores ceased to live at Meadows Mill, but according to Eastham parish records, members of the family were farmers in Orleton and Eastham well into the early 20th century.

By the time Thomas Moore emigrated to the United States, the coming of the railway to Tenbury and the Teme valley had sounded the final death knell to the majority of mills in the area, unless they could justify, by other work, the cost of maintenance of their weirs and machinery. Even so, Meadows Mill struggled on as a working corn mill until the 1890s. In the 1881 and 1891 censuses there was only one live-in worker/servant, however. The mill's 'fishery', or eel traps, first recorded in the Domesday Book, may still have provided a useful income for the miller and contributed to the local economy.

The mill's 17-ft diameter cast iron wheel, made and installed by G.Turton, Ironfounders of Kidderminster, in 1840, survived being scrapped for the war effort in both 1914 and 1939, but unfortunately succumbed to the scrap metal merchant for a few pounds in the 1950s.

Once a watermill ceased to operate, building and weir would soon deteriorate unless another use could quickly be found for them. It has been only in recent years that there has been interest in preserving such structures

*Rea Side farm, near Neen Sollars, with its mill on the right*

117

for purely aesthetic reasons. If the miller's house and mill shared the same building it would often survive as a home. However, most of those in the Teme Valley and its tributaries were separate small buildings, often away from a metalled road, so they soon collapsed with little trace remaining.

Meadows Mill was more fortunate; in about 1900 the shell of the building was converted into a summerhouse by the Wallaces, who lived in Eardiston House and owned much of the land and property in the area. Also, at about the same time, a hydraulic ram was installed below the weir. This is a powerful but very simple device by which drinking water was fed by a clay pipe from springs in Linkhill and close to Dumbleton Farm, via reservoirs above Whitehouse Farm, then down to Meadows Mill, where it was pumped to Eardiston House and much of the village. Traces of the reservoirs and a network of 2 inch mains can still be seen on the surface close to public footpaths.

The eel traps and the hydraulic ram continued to serve the local economy until the 1950s when Miss Isobel Wallace, the last family member resident at Eardiston House, died. In 1957 the estate was split up and sold piecemeal. At about this time, as more properties were connected to mains water, the hydraulic ram ceased to function. Also, the loss of mill pools, ponds and pollution had begun to contribute to the almost terminal decline in the eel population.

Then, sadly, in 1960 the spectacular horseshoe-shaped weir was largely demolished. At the time it was the practice of river authorities to canalise rivers and remove weirs in the belief that this prevented flooding. This may have been the case for the immediate area, which is farmland, but the current wisdom is that weirs mitigate against more serious flooding in the lower reaches of a river where lie cities like Worcester.

With global warming, droughts are now becoming more frequent and severe. The demolition of a weir causes a major lowering of the water table and can have a detrimental effect on crops and reduce still further the flow of a river in summer.

Following the death of Isobel Wallace, who had a picture window in the side of the Mill overlooking the river, it became derelict again and would have fallen into the river had it not in the 1980s been rebuilt and converted into a holiday cottage. In a small way it is still contributing to the local economy by bringing customers to hostelries and shops and encouraging people to take more holidays in the UK.

Will there ever become a time when Meadows Mill weir is rebuilt and fitted with a turbine to provide the locality with electricity with a surplus feeding the national grid? Perhaps even more farfetched, will there also come a time when fresh drinking water is at such a premium that the springs above Eardiston will again provide the village with water, and will the eels come back?

# Farming memories of Edwin Henry (Harry) Spilsbury (1889–1985)

My father was left a farm called Cheveridge at Tenbury Wells, and he eventually took possession of and farmed it. Cheveridge was a small farm, some 50 acres. It had quite a good house and good outbuildings too, with a hop kiln. There was a hop field and a considerable pasture, with a quantity of fruit trees, apples, pears, plums and damsons. Milk cows were kept and two horses were sufficient to cultivate the land. There was a cherry orchard too.

Father was farming successfully when he eventually fell in love with and married a Miss Annie Dorrell whose family were quite prominent and consisted of six daughters and five sons at the Venn Farm. Eventually two boys were born, Arnold the oldest and myself, Henry.

On the way to school in the spring we would see the farmers cultivating and preparing the land for seeding. At each end of the field the sower takes a half bushel measure, oval shaped to fit the body. There is a leather strap attached and a handle on one side. The measure is filled and slinging it over the shoulder and with several marking stakes along the field, with a sharp stride and grabbing the handle with the right hand, he scatters the seed, throwing it high in the air and spacing the markers as he proceeds. The field being finished it is then harrowed and packed with one of those steel serrated packers which had a wonderful ring when on the highway. The seed drill of course eventually took over.

As we walked to school at harvest time we would witness the labourers with a hook and sickle bent over cutting a swath across the field, while the women tied it in bundles. It was hard work and hard on the back bending over all day long, especially for the women, who after a day's work had to cook the supper. The grain also had to be stooked. However there came a time when a mechanical reaper was invented and would ease the load. This machine had a bull wheel and a six foot cutting bar. It had three arms on the reel which had a board on each with several six inch pegs in them, and it was so geared that they would sweep across a quarter moon table sufficient grain to make a sheaf, which still had to be tied by hand. When eventually a real binder was invented, there was one in our district and on a Saturday we went to see what we had no conception of, a machine that, we were told, cut the grain, elevated it and tied into bundles. And for the life of us we could not conceive of just how a knot could be made mechanically. But upon arrival here was the binder

*Top: a tip cart on an unknown farm*
*Lower: a seed packer known as a Cambridge Roll on The Hyde at Stoke Bliss*

proceeding and kicking out tied bundles. However the twine quite often made a few misses. It seems that at that time binder twine was quite faulty. It had knots in it and weak spots also, but the problems were finally overcome to the relief of the stooker who had to re-tie them. There was no bundle carrier which necessitated a lot of walking for the stooker.

In these times the threshing engine was stationary and the thresher and engine were transported from farm to farm with horses and set up by the grain

*Top: a mechanical reaper*
*Lower: sheep shearing. On the right is Mr Postans from Broomyfield Farm*

stacks. After getting a head of steam on the engine, hard coal was used to fire the engine, the engine starts with a toot of the whistle. The bundles are placed one at a time on a platform, when a man cuts the band and passes on lengthwise to a person who feeds it evenly into the cylinder which is a steel drum cylinder with steel slats attached. These slats thresh the grain out, and should there by chance be too much at a time, the cylinder, which had quite a pleasant hum, would then give quite a deep moan. When the straw came out at the rear end one would hardly know that it had been threshed, because the straw with the

# GINRIDDING,

### IN THE CHAPELRY OF KNIGHTON-UPON-TEME,

#### In the Parish of Lindridge, Worcestershire.

## To be Sold by Auction,

# BY G. WINTON,

## On Monday next, the 15th. of March, 1847,

### THE FOLLOWING ARTICLES OF

# LIVE STOCK,

### WITH SOME FARMING IMPLEMENTS,

### About 700 Gallons of Cider, Casks, 4 Sides of Bacon,

## HOUSEHOLD FURNITURE &c.,

### The Property of Mr. John Brown, at Ginridding aforesaid,

(WHO IS QUITTING THE ESTATE):—

Comprising 1 Cart Horse, and 2 Cows in-calf, narrow-wheeled Cart, Ell Rake and a variety of small Farming Implements; about **700 Gallons of Cider**, at—per Gallon, **4 Sides of Bacon**, 3 large Cider Casks, 8 Hogshead ditto, and a small Barrel, Tent and Stump Bedsteads, 4 Feather Beds &c., Sheets, Blankets and Bedquilts, 2-leaf Dining Table, Dressing ditto, Round and Square Tables, 3 Cupboards, Linen Chests, Dresser with Drawers and Shelves, Writing Desk, Parlour and Kitchen Chairs, Time-Piece, Glass and Earthenware, Fire Irons, Brass and Iron Candlesticks, Pots, Kettles &c.; Cheese Press, Barrel Churn, Milk Pans and Tins, Tubs, Pails and Buckets, Butter Mit, Bench and other Articles.

*\*\* The Sale will commence at 11 o'Clock in the Forenoon.*

B. HOME, PRINTER & BOOKSELLER, TENBURY.

*James James,*
*an estate carpenter*

head still on was quite intact, but with no grain whatsoever left in the head. The straw then went into an attached knotter and was tied in large bundles and stored in the barns for winter use. When travelling along the highway it used to be a common experience to hear the drum of a thresher. It was a pleasant sound.

The grain ran into those 225lb grain sacks and with the help of another man was lifted onto the back, when it would be carried up quite a number of stone steps and dumped on the floor of a granary. It was a strenuous job.

On going to school in the autumn, we would witness both men and women pulling

*The foldyard at Broomyfield, Hanley, east of Tenbury, in the 1920s*

swede turnips all by hand. They had a special heavy knife for the job and pulling them with their bare hands, they cut off the bottom root and the leafy tops, which incidentally were covered with frost, and threw them into piles. When they were covered with leaves the men's trousers and the women's dresses were soaking wet, and such was the hardy people's work of those times. But fortunately mechanisation has taken over just as it was with hop picking, where today they are picked mechanically. The turnips were then hauled by horse and cart to the farm yard, where they were piled in a row and covered with straw and then dirt, where they kept perfectly through the winter months. At that time they had, too, quite an economical way of harvesting these turnips. When they were full grown in the autumn, they would turn a flock of Oxford or Shropshire sheep in the field and they would first eat the top leaves off and then nibble away at the fleshy turnip until it was eaten right into the ground. This method saved a lot of labour and besides the sheep fertilized the land for future crops.

# Hop Growing

*Humulus lupulus* has been grown in the Teme Valley for centuries and has produced an industry that continues to the present. These are hops and their production in the valley has historically been equal to that in other parts of the country.

The Hop occurred naturally in many parts of England in ancient times but thrived in the wild among the hedgerows and the willows. Poor people ate the young shoots boiled as a vegetable before its potential in the manufacture of beer was known. The history of its development is as follows:

1511  The first known commercial hops were grown in Britain.

1520  Weavers from Flanders settled in Kent bringing with them new varieties of hops and knowledge of how to use them effectively in the brewing process. (An old adage says: 'Hops, Reformation, Carp and beer came to England the same year!', the Reformation starting on the continent in the 1520s.)

1524  Henry VIII outlawed the use of hops in the brewing process of ale, as it was thought they made people melancholy. (A Shrewsbury magistrate called it 'a wicked and pernicious weed'.) In 1552 Edward VI passed special legislation to permit the use of hops again.

1574  Reynolds Scott, the Father of English Hops, wrote the first definitive work on the English hop industry.

1710  Duty was imposed on hops for the first time.

1870  The area of hops under cultivation was almost 72,000 acres. A host of new varieties were developed including the celebrated Fuggle. Hops were grown in 53 counties including eight in Wales and five in Scotland.

1932  The Hop Marketing Board was introduced to exercise statutory control and to ensure a sheltered, if unrealistic market for producers.

1982  E.E.C. rules led to the disbanding of the Board and the introduction of independent producer groups for the marketing of English grown hops.

1997  In England two hundred hop farmers grew hops in a total of 7,526 acres spread across Herefordshire, Worcestershire, Oxfordshire, Hampshire and the South East. Mobile hop picking machinery was made available to hop growers.

Today in the Teme Valley many hop producers survive and west of Tenbury is a hop farm that claims to be the most northerly one in England and the only one in Shropshire.

## Hop Production

*Stringing hops*

Even today, producing hops is a labour intensive operation and requires attention almost all year round. Cleaning and tidying up the hop yard or fields (called a garden in the south-east of England) takes place in the winter months after the harvest, and in late spring and early summer months the restringing is done. Once the hops are growing, the young shoots are pruned and trained up the strings.

Edwin (Harry) Spilsbury (see the previous chapter) recalls how this work used to be done in the early twentieth century:

Some of the hops were grown on ash poles while other fields were grown on wire work. There was a special acreage set aside called a coppice for the purpose of growing ash poles. The small seedlings were planted

126

and in due time they grew to the point where they were about 4 inches in diameter at the butt, at which time they were cut and trimmed and hauled to the farmyard where there was a creosote tank. They were then sharpened and placed into the tank [see also p.107] which held about two feet of creosote and had a fireplace underneath which was fired with ash chips. And when fully treated they were hauled to the hop field and distributed along the rows, which had been previously fertilized with guano which is simply the droppings from seagulls and gathered in great chunks off the coastal rocks. It comes in fifty pound jute sacks. They also used what was known as shoddy which is simply rotted and decayed old rags, which originated from the men and their donkey carts who used to go along shouting, 'Any old rags, any bones and bottles today?' And thus old clothes were put to good use. This slag [fertiliser] came to the railroad stations in car loads and was hauled and piled on the farm. Incidentally there were a lot of buttons of various sizes and we used to see just who could get the most colourful and varied collection. This shoddy and guano made good fertiliser and was spread.

And to continue, the poles being spread, a man with a wedge-shaped bar with a handle on the top would punch holes into the ground while another man would thrust a pole in quite solid. The holes were sloped so that the poles formed a V shape. The poles all being set, a man with a ball of binder twine slung over his shoulder in a jute sack and with a long pole with an iron hoop on the top ran the twine through it and tying it to the pole started to weave it from pole to pole, and occasionally tying it solid in case of a break. This procedure being completed, the next job was to tie the growing vines to the poles. They used Rafagrass, a kind

*Alfred and Sarah Powis preparing hop poles during the Second World War*

of flat grass, and the vines then started to wind right to the top where they would bunch in clusters. The land was thoroughly cultivated in the meantime. Incidentally a hop root is quite similar to a dahlia root.

The next problem was blight. As the vines grew, blight would attack them and they had to be sprayed. For this purpose a solution was made of Quasha chips and soft soap. These chips when tasted were quite bitter. The mixture was made in a tank, possibly fifty gallons. The tank was on wheels and had a pump inside with steel pipes running along each side with spray nozzles on them. It was drawn by horses and when in motion there was a cloud of misty spray in the air and the bitter Quasha eradicated the blight but unfortunately it occasionally had to be repeated a second time.

More recently a programme of spraying has been used not just to control the constant threat of pests and diseases but also to combat the growth of weeds between the rows. These tasks are normally carried out by a small staff of full or part time local workers.

In the late 1800s and early 1900s and up to the Second World War thousands of itinerant workers descended on the Teme valley in early September to pick the hops. They were often women and children from the industrial areas of the West Midlands. They came for a working holiday to earn much needed money to subsidize the meagre earnings of the breadwinner back home whilst spending several weeks in the clean air of the countryside.

The hops at this time were picked by hand in the hop fields. Harry Spilsbury takes up the story again:

*Pickers ready to cut the strings*

They would arise and be in the hop field by eight o'clock. They picked into what was known as a crib which were made of four corner posts, oblong shaped and with ash poles running along the top and at the two ends and with a jute sheet sewn to the poles. It formed a belly, so to speak, into which the hops were picked. The poles were pulled by extra men and laid on the ground. Then the pickers would cut the vines off and placing them into the crib they started to pick. At noon they were measured, a bushel wicker basket being used which held about one and a half of a grain bushel. And this was where I came in – I kept books as to the amount of hops picked.

They were then placed into large jute sacks and hauled to the drying kilns (called oasts in south-eastern England). This process was repeated late in the evening, when they retired. Now at the kilns, three in all, two with cowlings and one with a fan driven by a stationary steam engine, the hops were hauled up and placed on a slatted floor, which was covered with coconut matting. The floors were possibly twelve feet from the floor where there was a red hot coke fire burning with an iron pan of sulphur burning. The cowlings on top of the kiln were about eight feet in height and shaped like an ice cream cone upside down and made of wood. There was an opening on one side in which there was a board flange about six feet long and with the wind blowing, it kept the back to the wind while the steam and sulphur escaped. With the larger kiln was a steel fan driven by steam for faster processing. There was quite a strong odour of sulphur fumes about the floor area and while the workers

*Women pickers* c.*1901*

got immune to it, any stranger coming round would be seized with a fit of coughing and sneezing and make a fast retreat. The drying process completed, the hops were, with a special scoop, pushed out and on to a large room floor in which there was a round hole about two and a half

*A contemporary drawing illustrating several stages of the process*

feet in diameter into which what was known as a hop pocket, seven feet by two and one half feet, was dropped through and cinched at the top with an iron ring. The hops were then pushed in and filled to the top, when a stout man would jump right in and pressing them down would start to trample them. And as the hops were gradually pushed in he would tread to the top. When it was released the top was sewn up and the process repeated. Eventually to speed up the process there was a steel geared press installed, and when in operation a man would crank a wheel sending the plunger down with a pressure that made the pocket protest with a stretching sound. And when these pockets were released and sewn up they were so hard that one could not dent them with a fist.

To complete these pockets the name of the owner had to be stencilled on them. A sample too had to be taken from each pocket for inspection by the buyers. With a sharp knife a sample was cut, four inches by six inches and four inches deep and was lifted out with two pallets and firmly packaged. And when all was completed it was a wonderful sight to see all the packets tacked up and ready for shipment.

In the meantime the pickers continued to pick. With the constant pick, pick, pick and constant standing it became quite monotonous. However they had a remedy for this because all of a sudden they would

*Hop picking c.1935. This might be a hospital crib, one from which the proceeds were donated to the local hospital*

start to sing. Yes, there were leaders who had wonderful voices and with all the rest they would sing many of the old favourite songs of that time, such as 'My Wild Irish Rose', 'Bill Bailey', 'Two Little Girls in Blue', etc. but the most pathetic of all was the one of the 'River Thames' which runs as follows:

'While London sleeps and all her lamps are gleaming
Many of her people now are gently sleeping
Some have no home and are gently weeping
While others seek the river side and jump into the tide,
Because they are too proud to beg or steal.'

This may not be correct, but thus they carried on.

Hop picking was a healthy and interesting occupation and it was known that even doctors' and dentists' wives came to pick for the sake of their health in an invigorating environment. The pickers got all the fruit that they required because the boys used to raid the fruit orchards close by and pick the choicest apples and a special jennet pear. And too, the fishmonger use to come twice weekly with his loud cry of 'fish, fish, all alive-o. Come and get them while they are fresh. One-a-penny, two-a-penny. They will soon be all gone.' And at noon there would be fires started and there would be the aroma of frying fish.

The Missionaries used to come occasionally and with a slide camera they would expound on the scriptures.

In the 19th century, before the advent of steam trains and other motorised transport, it is believed that many of the hop pickers from the towns around

*Hop picking in 1948 at Lower House Farm, Rochford*

the West Midlands travelled to the Teme Valley by canal narrow boats. They travelled down the Staffs and Worcs canals to be met at Stourport by the hop growers who provided horses and carts to carry them to their hop farms. Later, the pickers travelled by train to Stourport and other stations such as Tenbury and Newnham Bridge.

The conditions the pickers lived under were truly awful, as cowsheds, pigsties, stables and barns were quickly tidied up to accommodate the workers. There was little or no sanitation. In time, conditions steadily improved on most hop farms and in more recent times purpose-built barracks were provided for living and sleeping, with a separate open fronted building known locally as a 'shanty' for preparing and cooking meals.

Sometime during the 19th century many growers began employing agents who hired pickers on their behalf. Their duties included the selection and engagement of experienced pickers, to whom they circulated information on train times to and from stations, and sending lists of pickers to the farmers. Pickers preferred everything to be arranged for them, rather than travel to the hop growing areas and then find employment.

At the Moor Farm, Eardiston, a system of hiring pickers was organised by a local character called 'Granny' Aldridge who claimed to have been born in a hop yard. She was 4 feet tall, smoked a pipe and used awful language – but

*Hop picking at Field Farm west of Tenbury in 1933*

was known as 'The Boss'. She had more than 1,000 pickers under her and controlled more than 30 under-agents.

In 1905 a report from Dr Farr, a Government Inspector, praised the conditions for the hop pickers at the Eardiston Farming Company's barracks. About 750 adult pickers and 420 half pickers (children) were accommodated there. Most of the women were wives of artisans from Cradley Heath and neighbouring parishes. The group huts merited special praise together with the provision of 2 ozs of tea and 1 lb of sugar per picker per week. The sum of 6 pence was also allowed to each for Sunday dinner. Potatoes and vegetables

*Thomas P. Adams of Lower Rochford with his hops in 1930*

were given free and fruit allocated at the end of the hop picking season. A trained nurse was also engaged.

Audrey Jenkins, a local resident, was employed by The Eardiston Farming Company for many years. She recalled the daily soup dished out for all the pickers at the end of the working day that contained many wholesome ingredients including pearl barley, lentils, and split peas. These required soaking overnight and the following day the mixture was split into two batches and boiled. Carrots, onions and potatoes were added along with seasoning, meat and bones. Unsurprisingly a lot of stirring was required. The pickers were then allowed about a pint each.

The Black Country pickers were joined by local casual workers, gypsies or travellers and many other itinerants.

It was not uncommon for the hop pickers to arrive with no money in their pockets and at the end of the season go home with nothing. Many preferred to spend their hard earned money on drink, which in some cases had been paid for with subs from the farmer.

One such tale was related by Dave Hinton, a landlord at The Nags Head Pub at Lindridge. A Black Country character came every season for many years and frequented the pub every evening for his beer and 'fags'. He ran up a bar slate over the weeks but at the end of the season without fail he would settle up on his last night. However one year he never turned up. The landlord's thoughts were 'That's the last I shall see of him!' Lo and behold the following Sunday a taxi arrived in the pub car park, the picker got out and went into the pub and full of apologies paid his outstanding debts.

*Hop kilns at Kyrewood near Tenbury*

## The end of an era

In the years following the Second World War it became more and more difficult to encourage workers back to the hop farms. Many jobs were available in the industrial areas of the West Midlands and came with paid holidays. Many of the women also had full time jobs or remained in the employment they had begun during the war.

Finding labour became a major problem on the hop farms, so growers had to look for other alternatives. In the early 1950s growers slowly began converting to mechanical means for gathering and processing the crops. The whole of the hop bine was cut straight from the wires and collected on trailers drawn by tractors. They were then transported to the picking machines, which had elevators with hooks that picked up the bines. They were dropped into rotating blades which stripped the cones from the bines and dropped them onto a conveyor belt. Workers, often women with nimble fingers, would pick out and discard any unwanted stalks or leaves. The cones were then bagged and stored before the drying process took place.

## Afterthoughts

Anyone calling in for a drink at a local pub in hop growing areas can still listen to local characters reminiscing about 'the good old days' and how they loved the hop picking and working holidays in the countryside. Nostalgia makes us remember the good times but clouds over the harsh conditions many of them endured, such as sleeping on straw in rat infested, creaky old farm buildings with very basic toilet facilities, not to mention the sometimes unpredictable autumn weather.

They were tough, spirited and hard working individuals who got on with the job in hand. The memories are of the friendliness of their fellow workers who always seemed to be happy, laughing and singing, visits to the local hostelries, over-indulging and then having difficulty finding their way back to their living quarters. There are also tales of the prisoners of war, especially the Italians, who disliked working in the afternoons and to the dismay of the local lads, spent much of their time trying to charm the local girls.

Today, with just a few growers left, the Teme Valley is a sad image of how things were in the past. The growers that remain hope for market improvements and rely on just a few part-time workers who join the few full time employees to gather the seasonal but continuing crop of hops.

# Col F.A. Whinyates, a soldier's soldier

In October 1906, the *Tenbury Wells Advertiser* carried the following obituary:

By the death of Colonel F.A. Whinyates, of Berrington House, on the 19th of October 1906 the country loses one of the surviving veterans of the ever to be remembered Crimean war, whilst the town loses a gentleman who is held in high esteem and respect by all who had the pleasure of knowing him.

The deceased gentleman had been confined to his residence for some time, earlier in the year undergoing an operation, which at the time was successful and gave him relief. His illness was known but to a few, therefore it came rather sudden to the town on Friday morning, when it became known that the late Col. Whinyates had passed away on the Thursday evening about 9:30. The deceased leaves a widow to mourn his loss, for who great sympathy is felt in her bereavement.

Col. and Mrs Whinyates came to reside in Tenbury just over seven years ago, and though not taking any active part in the town's affairs, the late gentleman always evinced an interest in anything that was good of his fellow-man. He was a staunch Churchman and in politics a conservative.

As an officer in the army he was beloved by all who came under his charge, and was highly esteemed amongst his brother officers, his wise counsel being greatly missed when he thought fit to retire into private life.

A singular co-incidence with the deeply lamented death of Col. Whinyates, is that it occurred on the anniversary of the Balaclava Charge.

Francis Arthur Whinyates, third son of Major General Frederick W. Whinyates, Royal Engineers, was born on 18 November 1837. On 23 October 1854, he joined the Royal Artillery at the age of 16, and a few months later he embarked at Liverpool for the Crimean War and was present during the greater part of the siege of Sevastapol.

A year later, on the breaking out of the India Mutiny, he at once volunteered for service in that country, and was appointed to No. 7 Company 14th Battalion, R.A., and embarked with it in the *Sydney* screw steamer, reaching Calcutta on 25 October. On 29 October the company proceeded by bullock dauk [mail cart] to Allahabad, where it was converted into a field battery, receiving the necessary guns and horses, and on the night of the 31st marched to Cawnpore. Many of the horses were vicious and unbroken, and the men indifferent horsemen and inexperienced. Great confusion ensued. To help matters on, Lieutenant Whinyates dismounted the drivers of his division and took his place at the gun, driving the team throughout the night, an action which shows the keen soldier he was.

Under General Windham, Lieut. Whinyates was present at the Repulse of the Piquets on 5 December 1857 and the battle of Cawnpore on the next day, and the following year at the action of Futteghur on 2 January and the Affair of Kunker on 6 April. At Kunker, with the support of some infantry, he rode forward and captured one of the enemy's guns, notching it with his sword to establish its capture by the Artillery.

On 14 April 1859, he was appointed to E Troop, Royal Horse Artillery, and marched with it on 6th October into Cawnpore, to join the escort there assembling which was to accompany Lord Canning, the Governor General, on his progress through the pacified provinces, which occupied over four months.

On 7 July the following year, a severe outbreak of cholera occurred at Meanmeer. Seventeen men of the troop died, and from 1 September to the end of October he was called on, in addition to his staff duties at Meerut, to take command of a Battery of Royal Artillery, all its officers being either sick or absent.

In 1861 he returned to England and was recommended by the Adjutant General, Col. Charles Bingham, to the Commander-in-Chief for appointment to the Adjutancy of Royal Horse Artillery, Woolwich. Subsequently he was appointed by the Duke of Cambridge to the command of C Battery, A Brigade, and arriving at Peshwar in January of 1872, he took over his new command. After a period of nearly five years in India he returned to England in 1876. He retired from the service in 1881.

He received for his services the Crimean medal with clasp, the Turkish medal and the Indian Mutiny medal.

On 10 June, 1886, he married at Woolwich, Emma Sophia Caroline, third daughter of Colonel Charles Bingham, R.A. Deputy Adjutant, General Royal Artillery.

In later years, Col Whinyates wrote *From Coruna to Sebastapol, The History of 'C' Battery, 'A' Brigade (Late 'C' Troop) Royal Horse Artillery* in 1884 (republished 2004), and edited *Lieut Swabey's Diary* in 1895, and *The Services of Lt Col Francis Downman* in 1898.

# Tenbury Rifle Volunteer Company

In the latter part of the 18th century, Napoleon inherited the challenge to stabilise the French nation and twenty years of wars followed. The threat of a French invasion despite the presence of the British Navy was very real and led to a resurgence in membership of the old Militias and in the creation of new volunteer forces. There was no shortage of volunteers to the cause for wages were low, and many joined because of the offer of extra money.

The *Worcester Herald* for 27 August 1803 records:

> The inhabitants of the parish of Tenbury, with their accustomed loyalty and patriotism, have formed themselves into a volunteer corps of Infantry to the number of 170 men to be called the Tenbury Loyal Volunteers for the general defence of Gt Britain, in case of invasion or rebellion and have nominated Mr Ed Wheeler of Kyrewood to be Captain of such corps.

The uniform consisted of a scarlet coat with buff coloured facings and white breeches, a combination which may have given rise to their nickname of the 'bread and beef corps'. By the time Colours were presented to the Volunteers by Mrs Pytts of Kyre House in August 1804 they had each put in at least 30 days attendance.

The Volunteers were disbanded from the end of 1808 but reformed in 1859 under the impetus of William Norris.

The Volunteers took an active part in the community of Tenbury, their orders for assembling being printed in the local paper:

VOLUNTEER ORDERS
For the week ending July 24, 1886

Wednesday – Battalion drill; undress uniform; fall in at 4 o'clock p.m.
Sunday – Church parade; fall in at 10.40 pm. Helmets and waist belts, without frogs, to be worn.

E.V.V. Wheeler,
Captain Commanding.

## COMING OF AGE OF EDWARD VINCENT VASHON WHEELER Esq
## FESTIVITIES AT TENBURY.

... To Edward Vincent Vashon Wheeler, Esq. Sir – We beg to present you with the colours of Tenbury Old Loyal Volunteers, of which your great grandfather was captain and your grandfather ensign. The colours were made and presented by ladies of the neighbourhood, at Kyre House, viz., Lady Caroline Rushout, Madam Pitt, Mrs Rock, Miss Wood, Mrs Holland, and the Misses Pardoe. They were displayed when Her Majesty Queen Victoria (then the Princess Victoria), and Admiral Lord Nelson visited 'our town in the orchard,' and they have also been displayed at all subsequent events at Tenbury.

We wish you every happiness, and as the honoured representative of the officers of the corps we beg to hand them to you as a memento of the day of your majority, and as showing kindly feelings which have always existed between the Kyrewood family and the people of Tenbury.

*A piece in the* Tenbury Wells Advertiser, *Tuesday, June 10, 1879. (Tuesday June 3 was the date Mr Wheeler actually achieved his majority)*

Monthly rifle competitions were held for many years and the results were also faithfully reported in the *Tenbury Wells Advertiser*, as here for 31 August 1886:

RIFLE COMPETITION. – On Saturday the return match took place between the Tenbury and Ludlow teams, on the Tenbury range. The weather was all that could be desired, but the sun was somewhat troublesome, particularly at 600 yards, where the mirage was very misleading. A tent was erected on the ground where refreshments were provided by Mr R. Robinson, of the Rose and Crown Hotel. The contest was one of much interest and was thoroughly enjoyed by all who took part in it. The result was a victory for the home team by 134 points.

In 1887 the country began a year of celebrations in honour of Queen Victoria's Jubilee and the military played a large part. The following was reported in the *Tenbury Wells Advertiser* for 2 August:

TENBURY RIFLE VOLUNTEER COMPANY

Detail for the Week.

THURSDAY – Review at Worcester. Full dress. No haversacks to be worn. Belts and scabbards to be well cleaned. Water bottles to contain sufficient to last until drill is over. Fall in at 6.45 a.m. All rifles to be returned to the armoury on Saturday for inspection.

## VOLUNTEERS ON THE GUARD

A correspondence upon this subject is being carried on in the columns of the *Daily Telegraph*, and we notice the following contribution by a Worcester officer: -

While agreeing with 'An Old Volunteer' in deploring our present state of unreadiness, I cannot fall in with views as to the establishment of Volunteer Guards. The existence of Guards in our own and other armies has not been found an unmixed good, nor do they work so well that we should seek to reproduce them in the volunteers. I am convinced that their establishment would be most unpopular with the existing force, would stir up all sorts of jealousy and would seriously interfere with recruiting. As a workable alternative I would recommend that a certain percentage of men per regiment be enlisted upon an engagement rendering them liable to foreign service. These men would be up to the physical standard of the regular army, should on enlistment pass through a course of preliminary training, should attend a certain number of consecutive drills each year, and should be made to attain a higher state of efficiency than is now required from the ordinary volunteer. A small present payment should be made to them during obligatory drills and when called out for permanent duty, with deferred pay and pension on attaining a certain age, or completing a certain term of service. Upon these or similar conditions, I believe there would be no great difficulty in re-enlisting nearly 10 per cent of the present volunteer force – say 15,000 or 20,000 men – and the presence of these picked men would in nowise interfere with the force as now organised, but would tend to raise the average of efficiency in the whole body. – I am, etc

H. Goldingham, Lieutenant Colonel

1st Worcestershire. A.V.

Worcester, September 15

*A piece in the* Tenbury Wells Advertiser *for Tuesday, September 21 1886*

THE ANNUAL SUMMER PRIZE SHOOTING will take place on Wednesday. 10th August. Firing to commence at 12 noon. Kneeling at 200, prone at 500; 7 rounds each distance.

By Order,

E.V.V. WHEELER,

Captain Commanding.

THE VOLUNTEERS: On Monday evening, the 25th July, Major Adams visited Tenbury for the purpose of inspecting the Volunteers (B company) prior to the review which is fixed to take place on Pitchcroft, Worcester on Thursday, the 4th inst. The march past received special attention, and a feu de joi was fired, after which the men and officers repaired up on the hill to Kyrewood House, where an excellent and substantial repast was prepared by their much esteemed captain, and his mother, Mrs Wheeler.

141

The muster was a large one, and full justice was done to the good things provided. There present were Major and Adjutant Adams, Major Norris, Captain E.V.V. Wheeler, Rev. T.A. Smith (chaplain), Lieutenant Murray, James V. Wheeler, Esq, etc. The usual loyal and patriotic toasts were given and duly honoured in a way that only Volunteers seem capable of. In the course of the evening Major Norris referred to a visit of the company to Gloucester some twenty-five years ago, when the Tenbury Volunteers were complimented on their march past, and he was sure they would sustain their reputation on the coming 4th of August. – Major Adams, in the course of his speech, said in effect the Tenbury company were second to none in the battalion. Captain Wheeler, in replying to the toast of his health, said that it was necessary to observe military discipline, and although he might at times seem rather hard on the men, he was sure they would see it was for their good. In response to the toast, 'The Volunteers,' from J.V. Wheeler, Esq., Lieutenant Murray said that he would answer for the company to a man that they would support their excellent captain under all circumstances. The proceedings were enlivened by several songs contributed by Corporal Fuller, Privates Farmer and Wormington, and Bandmaster F. Worrall.

On the day, there was no doubt gratitude that haversacks were not required, given the temperatures and the hours ahead of them. The review duly took place on 4 August and the paper reported the event:

### THE REVIEW AT WORCESTER

The celebration of the Queen's Jubilee at Worcester by a review of the whole of the military forces of the county and the laying of the foundation stone for a statue of Her Majesty, by the Duke of Cambridge, took place on Thursday. Although Tenbury is situated at the extreme western boundary of the county, the interest evoked in the transactions at the county town was very general among the inhabitants, and about 250 persons (including Volunteers) booked from Tenbury station to witness the day's proceedings. The members of 'B' company of Volunteers presented a more than usual smart appearance on the morning of the parade, and it was apparent that the injunctions of their captain as to the state of their arms, clothing, and accoutrements had been carefully attended to. The company included non-commissioned officers and men, and was under the command of Captain Wheeler and Lieutenant Ross. Major Norris also accompanied them. The company, headed by their band, marched to the railway station, where they departed by the 7.31 train to Worcester. On their arrival at the 'faithful city' the men were marched on to Pitchcroft – the scene of the day's proceedings. Refreshments were partaken of, but the inferior quality of the bread and cheese served out to the men proved anything but an enticing bait, and called forth hearty anathemas for the 'contractor'. Soon after 11 o'clock the various arms of the service had taken up the positions allotted to them, and awaited the arrival of the Duke. The scorching rays of the sun beat down pitilessly upon the men, and Volunteers began to droop here and there from the fierce heat. The services of the stretcher-bearers were brought into use and as the men fell they were picked up and conveyed to the hospital tent, which was under the management of Surgeon-Major Hyde. About 28 Volunteers and 2 Militiamen were treated, all of whom revived after a short time. His Royal Highness the Duke of Cambridge arrived on the grounds a few minutes before 12, accompanied by Earl Beauchamp, General Lyons, and General Stephenson.

After the general salute the Duke proceeded to inspect the whole line. The march past commenced at 12.30, being led off by the Yeomanry, commanded by Lord Lyttleton. They kept excellent line. Next came the mounted party of the Artillery with their two guns and after them the band of the Artillery, followed by the corps, in eight batteries headed by Colonel Lyne. Following the Artillery came the 36th regiment, headed by their band and the fifes and drums of the Militia. The leading companies elicited much applause. The Militia, who followed, also received a popular ovation for their marching, the companies with the colours passing in good line, and being especially noticed by the Commander-in-chief. When the whole of the infantry had passed, they were massed at the south end of the Croft, and the cavalry, who had reformed, marched past in fours, their order being much admired. They then reformed the line and marched past at the trot. Then came the Rifle Volunteers in line of quarter column, this movement being scarcely so successful as their first. The Regulars and Militia next went past in the same formation, in excellent style. The Artillery marched past alone. Whilst the cavalry went through some other evolutions the infantry stood 'at ease'. The whole force then formed into review order, the Rifle Volunteers being on the left, the Regulars and Militia in the centre, and the Artillery and Cavalry on the right. This was the imposing movement of the day. The total force on the ground numbered slightly over 4,000 men, and at the conclusion of the movement they were formed into three sides of a square, and the Commander-in-Chief addressed the commanding officers. He said that nothing could exceed the excellence of the parade they had seen that day. It had been highly credible to the officers commanding and to the non-commissioned officers and men. He was glad to see the line regiment among their comrades of the county. Nothing could be more credible than the appearance of the Rifle Volunteers. – The troops then broke off for refreshments. The Tenbury company arrived home about 8:30.

And presumably a 'good time was had by all'! However, the matter of the men's meals lingered on. The following appeared in the *Tenbury Wells Advertiser* on Tuesday 9 August 1887:

# V.  R.

# B COMPANY,
## FIRST VOLUNTEER BATTALION
# WORCESTER REGIMENT.

## THE ANNUAL MEETING FOR

# PRIZE-SHOOTING

#### FOR PRIZES GIVEN BY THE FOLLOWING LADIES AND GENTLEMEN :----

| | | | | | |
|---|---|---|---|---|---|
| Major Norris | £3 | E. F. Williams, Esq. | £2 2s. | Rev. H. B. Hunt | £1 10s. |
| Major Wheeler | £7 | J. L. Sweet, Esq. | £2 | Rev. R. Wood | £1 1s. |
| Major Murray | £2 | Captain Hill-Lowe | £1 1s. | A. P. Bloome-Ansley, Esq. | 10s. |
| Captain Ross | £1 | S. C. Whitefoord, Esq. | £1 1s. | W. S. Davis, Esq. | £1 1s. |
| Lady Northwick | £4 | Captain Adams | £1 | | |

## Was held on August 23rd, 1894.

| | | £ | s. | d. | | | £ | s. | d. | | | £ | s. | d. |
|---|---|---|---|---|---|---|---|---|---|---|---|---|---|---|
| 1. | Sergeant Pope G. | 3 | 0 | 0 | 13. | Private Phillips W. | 0 | 14 | 0 | 25. | Private Davis W. | 0 | 5 | 0 |
| 2. | Lance-Corporal Anstis A. | 2 | 10 | 0 | 14. | „ Brockway G. | 0 | 14 | 0 | 26. | „ James J. | 0 | 5 | 0 |
| 3. | Sergeant Page J. | 2 | 0 | 0 | 15. | „ Parker R. | 0 | 13 | 0 | 27. | Sergeant Worrall F. | 0 | 5 | 0 |
| 4. | Corporal Tippins M. | 1 | 15 | 0 | 16. | Color-Sergeant Jeff J. | 0 | 12 | 0 | 28. | Private Blount E. | 0 | 5 | 0 |
| 5. | Private Turner J. | 1 | 5 | 0 | 17. | Private Bishop H. | 0 | 12 | 0 | 29. | „ Barrell F. | 0 | 4 | 0 |
| 6. | „ Knott J. | 1 | 0 | 0 | 18. | Coporal Taylor J. | 0 | 10 | 0 | 30. | „ Banfield W. | 0 | 4 | 0 |
| 7. | „ Ashley B. | 0 | 17 | 0 | 19. | Private Round W. | 0 | 10 | 0 | 31. | „ Robinson J. | 0 | 4 | 0 |
| 8. | Sergeant Rees W. | 0 | 17 | 0 | 20. | „ Fletcher J. | 0 | 9 | 0 | 32. | „ Round D. | 0 | 3 | 0 |
| 9. | Private Turford J. | 0 | 16 | 0 | 21. | Bugler Blount V. | 0 | 7 | 0 | 33. | „ Mills S. | 0 | 2 | 6 |
| 10. | „ Langford J. | 0 | 16 | 0 | 22. | Private Rippard J. | 0 | 7 | 0 | 34. | „ Brown J. | 0 | 2 | 6 |
| 11. | „ Phillips H. | 0 | 15 | 0 | 23. | „ Bufton W. | 0 | 6 | 0 | | | | | |
| 12. | Lance-Corporal Pope F. | 0 | 15 | 0 | 24. | „ James W. | 0 | 6 | 0 | | | | | |

FOR RECRUITS.—£1 will be given to the Recruit who proves himself the best shot in his Recruit's Course.   Winner, Private F. Anstis.

BEAUCHAMP CUP.—To the Volunteer who shall make the highest score at 200 and 500 yards in two of the Monthly Competitions and Summer Prize Shooting.   Winner, Sergeant G. Pope.

LADIES' CUP.—To the Volunteer who shall make the highest score at 200 and 500 yards in the Summer Prize Shooting.   Winner, Sergeant W. Rees.

### The distribution of Prizes takes place at 7-30 p.m. on December 24th, 1894.

## CONDITIONS OF PRIZE SHOOTING.

Number of Shots— Seven at each distance.

Position—Standing or kneeling at 200 ; prone at 500 yards.

No Volunteer shall be allowed to take more than one of the above Prizes, except the Beauchamp and Ladies' Cups.

Any member absent at the completion of the firing at the 200 yards' range will be debarred from shooting.

Each competitor must be efficient for the present year.

Attendance at Company Drill or Church Parade to count as 1 point, each attendance at an Adjutant's Drill to count as 2 points, each attendance at Battalion Drill to count 3 points, and attendance at Inspection to count as 4 points.

Any member appearing on Parade without his waist-belt and bayonet will have half a point deducted in respect of any such default.

TIES TO BE DECIDED AS FOLLOWS:—(a) By the score made at the longest distance in the competition.   (b) If still a tie, by the fewest misses.   (c) If still a tie, by the fewest outers.   (d) If still a tie, by inverse order of shots counting by twos from the last shot to the first.   (e) If still a tie, by inverse order of shots counting backwards singly from last to first.

Any member who is absent, except from sickness or by leave of the Commanding Officer, from the Annual Inspection or from any Battalion Drill, will be disqualified from receiving any of the above Prizes.

Each competitor to shoot in undress uniform.

### W. B. MURRAY, Major Commanding.

*'B' (Tenbury) Coy, First Volunteer Battalion Worcester Regiment*

Respecting the refreshments provided for the Volunteers and others at Worcester, there is quite a diversity of opinion as to what were the contents of the paper bags distributed to the men. One of the articles was unmistakeably the orthodox 'penny loaf', and the other article was supposed to be cheese and the men proceeded to appropriate it forthwith; but many became doubtful of the propriety of so doing, and left further analysis to the ragamuffins who were in attendance. Some suggested that it must be yellow soap, the matter is still an open question. – The pork pies, although somewhat 'out of season,' were well seasoned, and that is a great point in the manufacture of these doubtful concoctions.

Early in 1888 the paper was able to report:

WORCESTERSHIRE VOLUNTEER CORPS. – The annual Parliamentary return of the Volunteer corps of Great Britain for the year 1887 has just been issued. From it we gather the following particulars; The county of Worcester has two battalions of rifle volunteers; and in addition a brigade which is associated with the Welsh Division of Royal Artillery. The 1st Battalion has an authorised establishment of 1,212, and a roll of 1,179, four members being inefficient. The establishment of the 2nd Battalion is 809, and a roll 803, seven members ranking as non-efficients. The batteries of Artillery number 648, including 66 non-efficients.

And later that same year:

### VOLUNTEER ENCAMPMENT AT HAGLEY

For the first time since its formation, the First Volunteer Battalion Worcestershire Regiment have experienced a week's life in camp. The site selected for the camp was at Hagley Park, by permission of Lord Lyttleton. About 823 men and 42 officers went into camp on Saturday week, but in all some 1,069 men of the regiment had given in their names, and most of these joined the camp during the week. Twenty-four men of the Tenbury company left Tenbury on Saturday week for the camp, under the command of Captain Wheeler, and were joined by Lieutenant Ross.

During Saturday night the weather was very rough. Rain fell heavily, and the wind blew with such violence as to blow down the tea tent. Church parade was held on Sunday morning, when the regiment was drawn up in two battalions on the parade ground and formed into a square. The Old Hundredth hymn had been sung, a shortened form of Morning Prayer was conducted by the Rev. E.H. Winnington-Ingram, M.A., rector of Ribbesford, one of the acting chaplains of the district. The regiment was then formed into line at open order and inspected by Colonel Knight, who afterwards put them through a few battalion

NAME OF CORPS *1st V B Worcestershire Regt*
HEAD QUARTERS *Kidderminster*
DATE *14th December 1897*

# Certificate of good service

*No 98 C. Sgt J. Jeff*

Has · served · with · credit · from *18th Nov. 1859*
to · the · present · date · in · this · corps

He · has · been · returned *38* times · as · an · efficient · in

each · of · the · following · years · viz. *From 1859 to 1897*

He · has · at · his · own · request · ceased · to · be · a

member · of · this · corps ·

*Observations* *Promoted Sergt. 30.11.67. C. Sergt.*
*29.12.74. Marksman 30 years, at R at Queens Body 1567 + 8 Pot*
*St Georges Badge 1867 Three Bronze Medals & County Badge*

SIGNATURE OF COMMANDING OFFICER *R Falls Watson Colonel V.D.*

SIGNATURE OF ADJUTANT *Annimbloal Capt & Adjt*

*Note Here insert any distinction won by the Volunteer such as Number of times
Marksman, Winner of Queen's Prize, N.R.A. Medals, &c.*

movements. A good many visitors were present during the day, and the weather on the whole was fine. The reveille was sounded at half-past five on Monday, it being intended to have an early drill. Rain was falling heavily, however, and this had to be abandoned, the men keeping under cover of the canvas until after breakfast. The regiment paraded at 10.30, and had a two hours' battalion drill. A concert was given in the camp on Saturday night. Better weather prevailed during the remainder of the week, and the drills were continued daily without interruption. The athletic sports took place on Wednesday, and the weather being very fine a large number of spectators were present. Several teams competed in the Tug-of-War, which was won by Tenbury, who were captained by Sergt. J. Page. The team consisted of the following men: Corporal T. Badland, and Privates, E. Venmore, J. Rippard, T. Bishop, G. Wilden, and H. Page. In presenting the prize to the Tenbury team, Colonel Sir F. Win-Knight, K.C.B., said that he had noticed that since he had been in command of the battalion the Tenbury company had some of the tallest and strongest men in it and he had much pleasure in presenting the captain of that team with the prize, wishing they might always remain as strong as they had proved themselves to be that evening. The inspection of the regiment took place on Friday, and Saturday the camp was broken up.

The Tenbury company arrived home on Saturday, and, after partaking of refreshments at the Rose and Crown Hotel, marched to the armoury. Captain Wheeler, in dismissing the company, spoke in high terms of the conduct of the men during their stay in camp, and said that he had much pleasure in testifying to the fact that for general conduct and appearance the B company was one of the best in the battalion.

The Wheeler family had been associated with the Volunteers from its very beginning in 1803. This association remained even after the Volunteers were subsumed into the active Worcestershire territorial regiments in 1908. The following records, on 29 January 1889, a presentation to Major Wheeler.

PRESENTATION TO MAJOR WHEELER. – On Friday last the non-commissioned officers of the B company (Tenbury) Volunteers waited on Major Wheeler, at Newnham Court, for the purpose of making a presentation of a pair of military spurs. Inside was engraved: 'Presented to Major E.V.V. Wheeler by the Non-Commissioned Officers of the Tenbury (B) Company.' The presentation was made by Sergt. G. Pope, who said that they had called to beg Major Wheeler's acceptance of a pair of spurs and to congratulate him on his promotion, although the non-commissioned officers and men could not but be the losers by such promotion.

Major Wheeler said he had no idea what was in the wind until a very few days ago. He was very much obliged to them, and thought that their present was too good to wear; he thought he should hang

*'B' Company on Jubilee Day, 1897*

*Third row standing: Price, Tyler, ?, Price, Banfield, ?, Pope, Annis, Howells, Ashley, Wyer, ?, ?, Parker, Turner*

*Second row standing: ?, Bufton, Anstis, ?, ?, Lloyd, Bounds, ?, ?, Palmer, Rippard, Banfield*

*Front row standing: James, Griffiths, Taylor, ?, Turford (wears Kabul-Kandahar Star inter alia), Fletcher, Griffiths, Rounds, ?, Mullen, Anstis, Rounds, Griffiths, Colley, Parker, Myrtle, ?, ?, Taylor, Bishop, Parker (despatch rider), with Knott on his own to left of Parker. Dummy dressed in order for manoeuvres*

*Sitting on chairs: ?, Owen, Taylor, Tippin, Worrall, Page, Jeff, Capt Wm Norris, Dr Murray, Holder, Pope, ?, Mills, Taylor, Brockway, Blunt, Squires, Palmer, Rees (father)*

*Sitting on ground: Rounds, Bolas, Rees (son), Martin, Davis, Silley*

*E. Knott and W. James went to South Africa with the Volunteer Service Company in 1900. Knott died there of enteric fever. The names were given on sight by Mr Farmer in 1972, though he was only 8 when the photograph was taken*

them up to look at. In speaking of his promotion he said that he thought Lieutenant Murray would probably take the command in his stead, and that it was a matter of satisfaction to him that he could rely upon the non-commissioned officers to support their new captain as they had supported him. He (Major Wheeler) would still be amongst them, and he hoped still to see the same spirit pervading the Tenbury Volunteers which had made his duties as commanding officer a pleasure. In speaking of the Tenbury company in camp last year, Major Wheeler said they were the best behaved and most orderly company in the battalion. If anyone happened to suffer from exuberance of spirits, he had but to speak and perfect order was the result. In conclusion, he said that he should value their present, and assured them that he should not forget the Tenbury Volunteers nor the feelings which prompted such a useful gift. The deputation, numbering twelve men, were then invited to partake of a substantial spread provided by the gallant Major, to which ample justice was done.

During the years until the beginning of the Great War rifle competitions continued, as did camps, exercises and inspections.

In 1906 'B' Company (Tenbury) went to camp on Salisbury Plain. The contingent mustered 27 in the ranks led by Lieut Tapp accompanied by Lieut

*The Tenbury 'B' Company 1st Volunteer Battalion Worcester Regiment in 1880 with William Norris commanding*

*In 1907, on the last church parade as volunteers, some of the company
assembled outside the Pump Rooms where a photograph was taken.
Many of the men have been identified:
Back Row: Jim Lloyd, Morris, Jones, Mr Powis, Element, Reg Parker,
Mr Farr, Hartland
Among the Middle Rows: Ward, Jack Passey, Partridge, Wood, Jim Colley,
Horace Wakeman, Morris (Newnham), Harry Higgins, Ward, Mac Tupper,
John F. (Jack) Wheeler is third from the right
Seated Front Row: Frank Maund, George Pope, Mr Annis, Mr Gerald
Godson, Mr Tapp, Saunders, John Jeff, Bernard Ashley, Mr Watkins,
Walter Ashley*

*George Pope and John Jeff were long time members of the Volunteers and
are identified by their dark uniforms and long service medals. Both men were
very good shots, regularly winning or placing well in the rifle competitions.
John Jeff was also the Colour Sergeant and joined in 1859 when the
Volunteers were reformed. George Pope was a carpenter from the top of
Berrington Road. Mr Annis was a schoolmaster from Pershore who later
became Stanley Baldwin's agent. Mr Tapp lived at Woodhampton. Mr Watkins
was a schoolmaster at Newnham*

Godson and Sergt-Inst. Buttery. The Volunteer Band accompanied the men to the station. In 1908 local territorials spent a week in camp at Swanage in early August.

But by 1914 things had moved from the safety of exercises on home ground to the reality of war in France. One of the many casualties was Private John Frederick Wheeler, killed in France in September 1918. A year later his wife, Mrs E.N. Wheeler, went on a pilgrimage to the grave. The War Graves

*Tenbury volunteers for the Great War*

*Alfred Powis during the First World War. He was born in 1888 and lived at 7 Temple Meadow, Little Hereford*

Commission strongly advised her not to go but she went with her brother. Her journey is described in the next section. She took the cross from the grave and brought it back to Tenbury Church, where she had a brass plate affixed with the words:

Pte John Frederick Wheeler
2/5 London Regiment
Killed in action Messines
28-9-18
This cross was removed from
Pound Farm British Cemetery
Wolveghem

# A Widow's Journey to France, Sept. 1919

Extracts from the memoirs of E.N. Wheeler

After the war of 1914-1918 was over I had a great wish to see my husband's grave and the part of France where he had spent the last months of his life. The Imperial War Graves Commission ... strongly advised me not to go as there were no railway communications into that part of the devastated area of France and my journey might end in disappointment.

My brother had not been demobilised ... and I was so grateful to him for giving up his time ... [to accompany me]. At Boulogne we went through Customs and ... took the train to Calais – 3rd Class – and if you want to find discomfort in travelling try 3rd Class in a French train; no upholstery, narrow seats, the backs reach just above your head and you jolt and bump along and wish you had afforded a better seat. I don't remember much of that journey ... but I do remember the wonderful corn in the fields and my surprise that the French could grow corn as well as we could!

The next part of the journey was to St Omer and to Hazebrouck. We could see ... dumps of lorries, gun carriages etc. outside every station, not much cultivation the further we went, but small patches of beet and tobacco. It was dark when we reached Hazebrouck. This was the furthest reached by the Germans; we destroyed Hazebrouck and the guard of the train told us there was no hotel where we could stay but said he would take us to the café Leon. We followed him through the streets till we came to the café. He knocked loudly several times, but it was sometime before the door was opened by the landlord, a terrible looking old man in a great state of annoyance at being roused out of bed. He looked so villainous that we felt very uncertain as to whether we should not be the victims of some dreadful robbery with violence. However the nice guard had made us feel confident that he was to be trusted and we went in. The old man carrying a 'tallow drip' took us upstairs and just pushed us into our two rooms and left us. My brother came into mine bringing the home made cake my mother had provided us with and we ate it sitting on my bed and laughing at the thought of the poor old host and trying (at least I was) not to be nervous. We examined our beds and found they were very clean … In spite of this I couldn't screw up the courage to undress. My door would not fasten and there was no chair to put against it; nothing in the room but a bed and washstand. I lay on the bed looking up through a great hole in the roof to the heavenly blue sky and stars and I must have slept a little towards morning.

There was lots of noise early in the streets and I got up very early and watched the women hurrying along to shop, milk carts etc. and was glad when my brother came to say he was ready to go down. The old man looked less villainous than at night and there was an old woman several degrees cleaner than he was who brought us coffee and rolls, coffee in cheap blue and white bowls with very long spoons. It was a very cheap bed and breakfast and we then went to the station and got a train to Bailluel.

*J.F. Wheeler and his daughter Elizabeth*

The country here was almost all devastated … My brother remembered it was a fine town as big as Kidderminster and he had been billeted in 1916 in a large school then far behind the firing line. Now we saw a town completely destroyed and we spent some time along the cleared paths and talking to some English soldiers trying to find some way of getting to the cemetery. We looked into some of the rooms occupied by French people who had never left the town, rooms they had patched up with newspaper and blue sugar bags; they all seemed to welcome us and to be bright and smiling. One wondered how they could live in the place at all because so often we became aware of the most awful smell. Soldiers told us that a great number of horses and mules had been buried in the ruins – and people too.

Outside the town were huts where our men who were engaged in cleaning up the battlefields were living. We ... found the officer in charge and asked him if he had any lorry going in the direction of Wulverghem or Neuve Eglise. He told us the roads had been so shelled that no lorry could travel in that direction yet, but he told us we could walk it, about 10 miles ...

Though we had seen the destruction of town and village, yet it was nothing to what we felt at the destruction of the whole countryside. We walked along the cobbled roads, missing the shell holes; these were every few yards or so, all along the road – some really big, on the road and off it, filled with shiny stagnant water. There were bits of hedges in places but these had mostly been shelled away and in place of fields and cultivation nothing but long dry rough grass and only the broken trunks of trees. At one place we walked beside some wire netting still standing, about 8 ft high with camouflage still on it, smashed to pieces and then continuing again.

My brother, though he had been up and down the line in France and Flanders, said he couldn't have believed there could be such an awful scene of desolation. As he explained, during the war all the country behind the lines was full of activity, men and vehicles and movement. Everywhere now that was gone, and nothing to be heard but the rustling of the grass. We were glad when we got in sight of Neuve Eglise, a completely ruined village. It was above the surrounding country ... and as far as we could see, on all sides, nothing but the same devastation. Outside the village we stopped to photograph the Crucifix which, though everything was destroyed all round it, had yet never been destroyed. Near it were four or five graves marked by wooden crosses.

Then we went on to the village and found an 'estaminet' or inn which was one room, more like a cider house in one of our farms here than anything I can think of. We had bought some food in Hazebrouck and we ate it sitting on planks. We bought some grenadine; a sweet syrup, I thought very good indeed. There were about four peasant women in the

*J.F. Wheeler, daughter Elizabeth and wife E.N. Both this photograph and that opposite are taken in the garden of their house in Market Street, Tenbury*

room and they had stayed there all through the war. A young woman had a jolly little boy of two. I knew enough French to ask how old he was and his name, and although I couldn't understand all his mother said, she and the other women felt our interest and friendliness and we felt theirs. We soon set off again and when through the village came on a party of German prisoners of war with English guards repairing the roads. The guards seemed very pleased to see us and we stopped and talked a little and I thought the Germans looked pleased and friendly too. The next month they would all go back to Germany. That day in making their stretch of road, they had found four bodies which had been buried temporarily beside the road and the graves marked with a cross.

We now had a long stretch of repaired road, always cobble stones, but at last we came to a notice board giving the names of some cemeteries off to the right. Pond Farm British Cemetery was one of them. We walked along a path, most of the way on 'duck boards' … came to a larger [cemetery] that had Pond Farm on the gate. We found my husband's grave quite easily, a mass of weeds like all the others. We did a little tidying … and looked … to see if there were any other familiar names, but there were none … and we set out.

… all day we could hear guns; the shells collected on the battlefields were being exploded so that we were reminded in some degree of the sounds as well of the sights of war. Everywhere we walked were empty cartridge cases and we even picked up one or two live ones.

As we walked we became aware of smoke coming towards us and very soon clouds of it were blowing across the road. The firing of the guns must have set the dead grass alight and my brother thinking there might be some ammunition which might explode … made me run until we were clear of the smoke.

We met just outside the town [of Bailleul] an English soldier who told us of a YMCA hut where we should get tea and very thankful we were to hear of it. It seemed wonderful in that awful place to find anything so clean and bright and shining as that hut and the English woman in charge was just the type that we should like to represent us in a foreign land. We had tea and bread and butter and nothing ever tasted better than the tea.

# Mrs Hewitt recalls Tenbury

These memories are taken from a tape recording made *c*.1990.

### Mr Godson and Mr Wheeler

My husband was a plumber and Godson sat in this room and my husband said 'I'm very sorry Mr Godson to hear you are giving up the Council.' And Mr Godson sat here and looked at both of us. 'Well,' he said, 'I'll tell you why.' He said, 'We've always had a Council that has had nothing to do with politics. All we were interested in was the good of the people of Tenbury. I won't go to a meeting to be shouted and sneered at by the creatures who are putting themselves up for the council now.'

He was as straight a man as you could have found. He really was. He died in '64. He left [an estate of] three quarters of a million and all … was sold off. All those houses down Berrington Lane, which … sell these days for £50,000 were bought for £400 each.

[Mr Godson] had no children of his own but he had … a brother who lived over by Hereford and worked in London and his sister, Vera, used to come here often. Anybody who runs down Mr Godson in my hearing, they get an earful.

Most of the people in Tenbury now never knew him or anything about him. Not Gerald Godson, but his father before him set up the trust to help people to emigrate. That

*Gerald Godson at his home, The Court, circa 1955*

157

was a Tenbury Charity and then there was the Baylie Charity and that was to help if your children passed their scholarship and went away to secondary school. Anybody who couldn't afford it could apply to that for the children's education.

They would pay for children who had left school to be apprenticed. Not many people apply nowadays.

[My husband was born in Cornwall House.] My husband's grandfather – they came from Leicestershire about 1870 and he came first of all and

*Top: The Court when it was up for sale in 1962*
*Lower: The house being demolished later in the year. On the left is the*
*Bath House, built in 1840 to utilise the new found mineral water*

158

had an antiques business in Market Street ... and then they moved up to Cornwall House. It was a very large builders' yard and they built nearly all of Berrington Lane – council houses and everything. Even today they will tell you that those council houses along the Bromyard Road that we built – there is less money spent on them than any houses in Tenbury – they were well built and so solid.

E.V.V. Wheeler – you know Wheeler Orchard, well that was named after him. When he was on the Council and that piece of land came up for sale, he bought it for £100 and until they wanted it, it was let out each year and a friend of ours kept sheep on it. After the war it was decided to build on it and Mr Bostock, who was the Clerk at that time, he said to me, Mrs Hewitt, how am I going to work out the value of that land because they are going to put the houses on it, you see. And I said, 'It will cost £100 and you have had three times that back in rent, so you are on the credit side already', but at the present prices, I expect you would have to pay £100,000 for it.

When you met either of them [Godson or Wheeler] they always spoke. They never passed anybody by.

**The Second World War**
We got married here in Berrington Lane in 1940 and I've lived here ever since. The bungalow was built in 1934 and Mrs Banfield's, next door, was built in 1936.

We had a tremendous number of evacuees in Tenbury. There were evacuees from all over the place. Where the Catholic Church is now, there was a beautiful old house called 'Norville'. Capt. Avery and his wife, he was retired from the Navy, came here in 1938 – very nice people. When war broke out he was called back up, so they moved and a Catholic boys' school came there. They had boarders because it was quite a big house which you could turn into classrooms and dormitories. Some lived with Mr Ashley, where George Bedford lives now.

A French family lived there and the children went to the Catholic School and then Burford House, that was another evacuee school. That was Miss Kennett; they came up from Dover Court – down by Dover. They had Burford House and the house just below here where Mr Carter lives now. They brought their teachers and their own children with them. They also used the building at the back of the Violet Morris house which had been used as a dancing studio. That was used as an extra school room for the children.

The old Parish Hall had a school from Birmingham.

The *Tenbury Wells Advertiser* for Saturday 7 October 1939 gives fuller details of this last school:

The Tenbury Parish Hall will open on Monday as an auxiliary school, to be used by the 50 to 60 evacuated school children from St Augustine's Roman Catholic School, Birmingham, who are billeted in Tenbury and district. The hall has been divided so as to form classrooms for the children, who will receive instruction from the two sisters, who are in charge of them, and two lay women. Normal school hours will be the order – 9 to 12 and 1 to 3. The children have been given the use of the Tenbury Vicarage garden as a recreation ground.

# The Regal Cinema

One of the gems of Tenbury had its origins in moving pictures. Films first came to Tenbury in 1917 when the Corn Exchange was converted to show them. At the Tenbury Petty Sessions, Samuel Mattock, proprietor of the Royal Oak, applied for a cinematograph license on behalf of George Simpkin of Smithfield, Birmingham and Edward H. Stubbins of Rochford. The magistrates at the time were Col. Wheeler (chairman), Major Prescott and Mr H.T. Nott. Police Superintendent Walker asked that in addition to the usual restrictions there should be no performances on Sundays, Good Friday or Christmas Day. The chairman said that subject to police approval of the apparatus and building, the license would be granted.

The *Tenbury Wells Advertiser* described the opening night as follows:

> The new Picture House was opened on Monday night at the Corn Exchange Hall under circumstances that must have been gratifying to the promoters. The crowded audience could scarcely recognize the Hall in its festive dress. The walls were almost hidden by its gay bunting and other decorations, whilst the windows were covered with red blinds on which were pictures of well known Cinema stars. A small orchestra supplied a sympathetic accompaniment as the various films were shown and also entertained the audience during the changes.
>
> The seats were well arranged, three rows of tip up chairs were reserved for ticket holders. The pictures embraced a wide field of subjects both educating and interesting – the chief film being the *Goose Girl* (starring Margaret Clark) which was much appreciated. *The Story of the Great War* (part one) was very effective, cheers repeatedly greeting the pictures of our brave Allies and the *News of the Week* was equally well received. The object of the promoters is to provide a healthy and interesting enjoyment for the people of Tenbury District and if this week's performance is to be a criterion, they have certainly succeeded in their objective.

Times of opening were Monday, Tuesday, Thursday and Saturday 6:30 to 7:45 pm with a Tuesday matinee for those living at a distance. Admission prices were: tip up chairs 1s (5p), front seats 6d and children 6d.

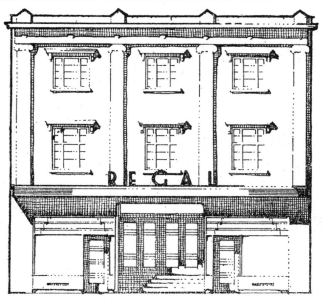

WORCESTERSHIRE'S NEW LUXURY CINEMA.

# REGAL

PHONE 100    **TENBURY WELLS.**    PHONE 100

## Grand Opening Thursday, July 29th, at 7-30 p.m.

CICELY COURTNEIDGE AND ERNEST TREUX
—in—

## Everybody Dance

LAUREL AND HARDY
—in—

## THEM THAR HILLS

COLOUR CARTOON.——GOOD LITTLE MONKEYS.

THE REGAL is air conditioned for your health and comfort and now just ventilated; the only plant of its kind within a radius of 20 miles.

PROGRAMME commences—Monday, Wednesday, Thursday and Friday at 7-30. Tuesday 2 p.m. and 7-30. Saturday and Bank Holidays 2-30, continuous from 5-30.

FREE CYCLE PARK at rear of Theatre. Earphones for the deaf. Free Car Park at Messrs. Edwards, Russell and Baldwin's Parking Ground, near Theatre.

Prices of Admission :—

Balcony 1/6 ; Stalls 1/3 ; Centre Stalls 1/-Front Stalls 6d.
BARGAIN MATINEES AND REDUCED PRICES FOR CHILDREN.
*Monthly Programmes posted to patrons leaving name and address at Box Office.*

162

## The Regal

With the coming of the era of purpose built cinemas, the Corn Exchange was replaced by the Tenbury gem, the present Regal, built in 1937. Mr J.N. Robson of Craven Cinemas Ltd had opened a cinema in Craven Arms and bought a site in Tenbury occupied by two shops owned by W.A.B. Ashley. Ernest Roberts of Birmingham, a specialist cinema architect, designed the building, which was completed at a cost of £12,000. The frontage was described as 'low key' in keeping with the historic town, and included two small shops, one of which now houses the Tourist Information Office.

The building has been listed as a site of Architectural and Historic Interest (Grade II) as it is a very rare survival of a cinema designed for a small market town. The schedule in the Grade II list notes that most of the original features apart from the canopy have been retained. In the foyer in its original position and livery is the art deco pay booth in green, gold and brass. The auditorium has its original entrance screen and fold-up usherettes' seats but is best noted for its murals of Mediterranean scenes with imitation canopies, realistically painted, over the projection portals in which design the sidewall ventilation grilles are cleverly incorporated. The projection room, reached by steep steps from behind the pay booth, still houses many very large pieces of equipment of the period.

There was a rumour that the murals were painted by Italian prisoners of war, but in fact they were the work of George Legge at the time of the original 1937 building. It is said that the vicar of Tenbury, Rev. Chesterton, visited while George was painting. He observed that there was no portrait of himself in the murals, so George obliged with the face of an ape! Murals were once common in cinemas but this is the most complete set known to survive in an auditorium.

*Some of the murals in the Regal*

163

Over time, the stage has been considerably enlarged at the expense of some seating so that live performances could be held. A community centre was built on to the rear of the cinema and linked to it, to provide additional meeting space for the town and to create dressing rooms for the theatre.

The film shown at the Regal's opening on Thursday 29 July 1937 was *Everybody Dance* with Cicely Courtneidge. The plot involved Cicely as the queen of London's nightlife being entrusted with the guardianship of her sister's two children. The children's grandfather, considering Cicely unsuitable for the task, tries to get them back. After many vicissitudes and song and dance numbers, everyone is reconciled and they obey Cicely's command to dance!

Also on the bill was the film *Them Thar Hills* with Laurel and Hardy and a cartoon *Good Little Monkeys*. One can presume that the mural monkey was happy with the choice.

Through the war years and just after, the Regal was managed by Mr A.J. Smith with Cyril Cook as chief projectionist. There was a programme change on Mondays and Thursdays with matinees on Tuesdays and Saturdays. There was also a continuous show on Saturdays from 5 pm so that people could come and go to suit the bus timetable. Sunday shows were introduced in the early 1950s. Admission prices were 2s 9d, 2s 4d, 1s 9d and 1s 4d. The Saturday matinee was 6d.

The cinema was one of six owned by Mr Robson. Films were booked by Mr Robson's main office – the latest releases were too expensive to hire so audiences usually had to wait a year for these films. Only old films were shown on Sundays.

Tom Dallow started at the Regal as a part-time projectionist in 1951 – by then Cyril Cook had taken over as manager. Tom worked until 1954 when he was called up for National Service. He resumed as a full time projectionist on his return, becoming part time in 1961 when he started work at Richard Lloyds.

Romance had blossomed at the Regal as Tom married Margaret, an usherette. Tom remembers using two projectors to ensure continuous showing as films at the time had five reels, which had to be changed during the performance. Dots on the film warned the projectionist when a change was imminent.

In those days the films contained nitrate, which was very flammable and one fire in the projection room burnt off all the plaster.

In 1966 the cinema was closed and remained derelict until the Town Council purchased it in 1969. It was then discovered that the murals had become detached from the underlying surface — strips of paint were gradually peeling off and hanging down. As this was deemed a fire risk, the council was advised that the building could not be used until all the paint was removed.

Frank Crisp, through his company, Management Consultancy Centre, had arranged for a group of local unemployed youngsters to be trained and their skills used on the refurbishment of Goff's School building which was then being converted into the museum. Frank therefore arranged for the same group to renovate the walls of the Regal, using an artist who had completed similar projects in Ludlow as the supervisor for the project. First the murals had to be recorded to show how they appeared when created. Then, with scrapers, scaffolding, ladders and acrylic paint the old murals were removed and copies painted in their place, a task which took three months. Sadly, the name of the artist in charge of the work has been lost.

*The Regal as it looks today*

165

In 1971 a friend of Tom Dallow's ran the cinema for a while and later a volunteer group called the Ace of Clubs managed it. The Regal was then handed back to the Town Council in July 1977 until the Wall family took over in 1986.

The Regal is still owned by Tenbury Town Council, a rare example of municipal cinema ownership. It continues as a cinema with showings of the latest films and at times is taken over by the Tenbury Operatic and Dramatic Societies for stage performances. Festivals hold band and pop concerts regularly as part of their programmes. As the largest venue in the town it is also used for public meetings. The most notable recent event, perhaps, was a public meeting to protest at the downgrading of Kidderminster Hospital before the election of 2001 when the Regal was filled and the overflow had to be accommodated in the Community Centre behind.

The Wall family ran the Regal until 2007 and continued to charge remarkably cheap admission prices. The Regal is now run by a volunteer group led by Bob Bydawell.

Managing a cinema is complicated. Showing the films and keeping the cinema clean is only part of the work. Films must be hired from one of about twelve distributors who usually require a deposit of £500 before they will supply films. The number of tickets sold has to be notified to the distributor after the showing, as the hiring fee is based mainly on attendance. Carriers have to be hired to deliver and collect the films, which must be insured. Advertisements have to be placed in newspapers and film programmes sent to people on mailing lists. With all these costs, it can be a struggle to break even.

Sadly the Regal was badly flooded in July 2007 and it will be closed for some time for renovation.

# Tenbury in Wartime

Jim Froggatt, Doug Powis and John Tetsall recall aspects of the defence of the area in the Second World War. First, Jim:

Two of my brothers died in plane crashes; one in Italy and one here at Hillwood. Others were cherry picking at the time, and I was hay making. (We picked 26 tons of cherries the year before.) On 23 June, Tony was in his Mitchell Bomber. Because he had only just joined the squadron it was felt that he should have a fly around to get used to his plane before going out with the squadron. He decided he would come up and visit us at the farm. Just across the cherry orchard was a dingle and it is assumed that he hit an air pocket that dropped him slightly; the tip of the propeller caught the chimney – only about 3 inches. It broke the propeller off at the boss and the vibration threw the engine out of its bedding and he had no chance with the weight coming off one wing. The plane flipped over and went as far as Eastham Church, crashing by the side of the river.

I rode a horse straight down to the crash at Eastham Bridge. It was all in flames and the ammunition was exploding.

## The Home Guard

The Home Guard were very inventive. There was a Sunday manoeuvre in which the Home Guard were set the task of the capturing the 'enemy' headquarters. They got Mr Drew's lorry from Newnham Bridge and put some barrels in the back. The Home Guard chaps got in these barrels and were driven straight to the headquarters, and being as he was a local chap nobody bothered to stop him. They all jumped out and captured the headquarters.

*Jim Froggatt*

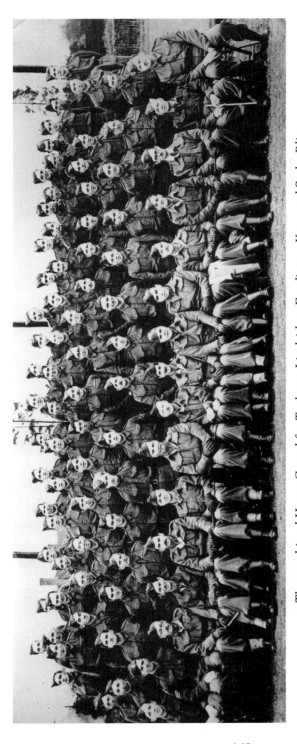

The combined Home Guard for Tenbury, Lindridge, Eardiston, Kyre and Stoke Bliss

Fifth row: ?, ?, ?, ?, ?, ?, Geoff Handley, ?, ?, Bert Yarnold, John Adams, Joe Dermills, ?, ?, Bill Kite
Fourth row: ?, ?, ?, Frank Worrall, George Rudd, Frank Vobe, Bill Vobe, Ernie Ryder, Bill Kennett, Eric Cooper, ?, Fred Hay, Reuben Martin, ?, ?, ?, ?, ?

Third row: Ernie Ertment, Arthur Allen, Jack Cox, ?, Alan Mason, Fred Pitt, ?, Eric Coombes, ?, Charlie Hartland, H. Wall, ?, ?, George Noble?, ?

Second Row: ?, Johnnie Powell, Ivor Mitton, ?, ?, Richard Robinson, Cliff Johnson, Jim Vobe, Fred Vobe, ?, George Bowkett, L. Chambers, ?, ?, Davies, Tom Wildblood

Front row: Reece Davies, Sgt Viles, ?, Eric Lowe, ?, Jack Higginson, Ivan Riley, Jim Nott, Harry Bentham, Dr J.E.B. Williams, Guiness, Bob Baker, Wilfred Morgan, ?, ?, Pearce

(John Tetsall recalls that the headquarters of the Home Guard was at the Tally Ho on Broadheath. They also used the Old Police Cottage because they had an advantage of height to see what was going on.)

## On the Farm

We had quite a lot of Land Army girls – four that lived in the cottage up at Hillwood – and they worked on a regular basis.

We had a chap on the farm who was a bit funny one way or the other and he took a shine to one of these lasses. She obviously took a shine to him. 'Oh Arthur, what about you taking me for a walk and showing me the countryside on Sunday night?' He told me all about it and I said he wants to take her down to Death's Dingle. It would be nice and quiet. Anyway he takes her down to Death's Dingle. 'Arthur, the gnats are getting up my legs, can you come and get them down for me?' 'I think it is about time we went back home,' he said.

Another time father took them to stook some beans, which had been cut with a binder. They do take a bit of telling which is the butts and which the tops and these girls stooked them all upside down.

We also had German PoWs. One, called Van Proft, was billeted at the farm at Hillwood and stayed until the end of the war. Another was a fighter pilot. He was an educated lad and was in the Nazi Youth Movement; he was brought up as a real Nazi, indoctrinated completely. He spoke quite good English but

*Tenbury Platoon of the Home Guard in 1943*
*Back row: P.Allen, ?, ?, ?, ?, Harry Wall, ?, ?*
*Middle row: Fred Pitt, ?, Richard Robinson, ?, ?, ?, ?, ?*
*Front row: Cliff Johnson, ?, George Bowkett, ?, ?, ?, Pearce*

169

just did not know how other people looked at things. He only saw it from the regime he had been brought up in, but he soon learned that there were other things in life.

*Two Italian PoWs*

We also had Italians and conscientious objectors. They were all sat in the granary one day having their lunch when the supervisor came out. He put them all round the cherry orchard getting the thistles down. They complained about it, but the supervisor said they worked just about fast enough to make a bloody scarecrow.

Doug Powis' wife Kath Hamer adds: We had conscientious objectors working on our farm. They came from Mountain Ash in Wales and … gave a concert at the Baptist Chapel. The woman who played the organ said to the conductor, 'You haven't got that right.' He replied 'Madam, if you played what was on the music you would know I was right.'

Two Land Army girls came to Field Farm where they did threshing and potato picking. Some farmers abused them by giving them work that was too hard for them. Girls were issued with clothing and they were very good workers. Some stayed on and lived on the farms during the war.

Father was on the War Ag Committee and was the instigator of Oldwood Common being ploughed to grow corn. The War Ag had its headquarters by the entrance to Kyre Park. John Tetsall remembers that this was where tractors and other implements were stored for farming. The War Ag issued tractors and ploughs with their own drivers and if a farmer was behind with cultivation he would get in touch with War Ag and they would come out and get him up to scratch. They had Agricultural Officers and you had to be up to time with planting. If you weren't capable of keeping up to time they had the powers to push you off that farm and put somebody in to do it. They used to come around twice a year inspecting your farm for cleanliness.

Doug Powis joined the Fire Service of which he has some memories:

## The Fire Brigade

George Maund was Chief of the Fire Brigade and in 1943 when I was 17 I joined the Auxiliary Fire Service. As I could drive they made me up to Fireman. There was a control room on Teme Street with two bunk beds and two women were on duty all the time.

There were six of us on duty as firemen; all part time. We had a red fire engine, the major trailer pump, and in the yard at the back there were two cars with lighter trailer pumps behind. There were also three cars converted to ambulances.

There was a hose drying tower and a siren made from four motor horns. I had a tin hat, tunic and trousers, Wellingtons, leggings, shoes, great coat, gas mask, belt and axe and a belt line to tie to a ladder and two blankets and a kit bag. We were on duty from 8 at night until 8 in the morning; one day every six days. I got paid 4s a week. We had a big hut built in the auction yard as a rest room for the firemen. It was a wooden hut with two stoves and there were two full time firemen on duty all the time. There were three of us from Maund's Garage who were in the fire service and they were Harold Preece, Bill Carver and myself.

Doug also recalls a host of other details, such as that Tenbury equipped a whole ship's crew. A balaclava, mitts, sea boot stockings, night shirts were all provided. Even school children knitted for the project. Also that valuables stored in the bank at Tenbury were sent to Batley in Yorkshire for safe keeping, and that the chap who worked at the gas works had a gas-propelled old type Austin 10 with a big bag for the gas on top of the car.

Later in the war he remembers the Americans, who were based in transit camps down the A49. They used the new bypass at Church Stretton as a parking area for their tanks. The bypass wasn't in use then. They had to grease the roads to get the tanks around the corner of Ludford Bridge and Temeside in Ludlow.

John Tetsall remembers his time in the ARP (Air Raid Precautions):

I was employed on the farm. It was a reserved occupation but we had to do quite a bit of civil defence and I was in the ARP.

We didn't see much here, but one night they lit Oldwood Common by an incendiary bomb. One other night I was just going home after 12 o'clock when I heard this plane coming over and it was an enemy aircraft and suddenly everything lit up. They dropped one at Stockton. They said he was following a Yarranton's bus because it used to take workers from this area to a munitions factory at Hereford. It was following the bus but the bomb just missed it and it made a crater. It cut a holly tree in half. (Jim Froggatt's recollections are slightly different, he thinks that bombs were dropped at the top of the Road Bank, up the Boraston Road and Low Bank at Stockton where the S bend is: 'They were unloading some hop-pickers from a bus and I expect they were causing a bit of light. They also came down at Yarnold's of Gritthill. Yarnold was out with a hurricane lamp and he heard them coming down and jumped in a ditch. They hit the fowl house so it was well on target'.)

171

I didn't get issued with a tin hat or a gas mask. I didn't get issued with a beret or a uniform. The overcoat never arrived nor did the shoes. They got picked up en route I expect.

If there was an emergency we had to leave our work, otherwise it was all after work. This area was dead quiet and we were never called out in the daytime. We had meetings at night about once a fortnight.

The Chief Warden from Tenbury used to come out in his 1938 Morris Tourer (Morris eight) and demonstrate various things. He was demonstrating a phosphor bomb. He had a length of galvanised tubing and the oil bomb in a bottle. 'Everyone stand back,' he says, 'because this thing flies.' He drops it over and smashes the bottle and everything went up. He was telling us all about it when someone said, 'Harold, have you a car? Because it's on fire.' He had about five buckets of sand in there a bit quick. It set the tar alight in the road!

Gas was demonstrated. We had nose irritants and tear gas. Mustard gas wasn't demonstrated because we didn't have strong enough gas masks. Also demonstrated were skin irritants. We were issued with little tubes of cream to use if we got it on our skin. They didn't tell you that they were doing this, but someone came round the back and loosed one off.

There were one or two private air raid shelters but nothing issued. One person had one built in a coppice, but if there was a raid he had to run about 500 yards.

**Local defence sites**
Putting their memories together, Jim, Doug and John think that there were searchlight batteries at Birchley Farm, Bockleton, opposite Kyre School, one as you came down Hatchbank at Bleathwood, a site at Woodston near Lindridge and another at Stoke Bliss. The base camp was in the area of Pensax Court where there was another site. Jim used to drive a lorry to Newnham Station where two soldiers loaded coal and took them around the searchlight batteries. Woofferton was also fairly well guarded with searchlights and anti aircraft guns, whilst at Greete there was a radar research place, near the Round Oak.

There was a pillbox down at Eastham Bridge – a square brick structure attached to the bridge on the downstream side. They put big concrete blocks by the side of the road to be moved into the road if required. They can still be seen on the New Road by Eastham Grange. Across the bridge there was a series of square holes into which metal rails could have been inserted to help form a road block. The holes had just a little cover over them. Stanford Bridge also had a pillbox and Tenbury had one.

# John Patrick Kenneally VC

John Kenneally won the Victoria Cross in the Second World War, but he wasn't exactly who he seemed to be.

Leslie Jackson was born in Birmingham in 1921 and attended King Edward's School, Fiveways, under one of the free scholarships available for boys of poorer households. He excelled in sports and represented the school in athletics and swimming. He also joined the Cadets where he learned to shoot and put on puttees properly.

He admitted that he matriculated in 1938 by the skin of his teeth, and initially worked at small mundane jobs, which he hated. Then he went to work at a petrol station and took on responsibility for organising shifts and booking in work.

In 1939, with the talk of war, he and his friend 'Tipp' (Albert Tipping) saw an advertising campaign encouraging men to join the Territorial Army (T.A.). They both signed up and in basic training learned drill, physical training, map reading and arms. With this concluded, they were offered either the T.A. Battalion attached to the Royal Warwicks or a T.A. Battery of Royal Artillery. On reaching 18, Leslie followed advice from his boss and took the Royal Artillery option, learning about 25 pounder guns.

In the first half of 1939, both young men were posted to Barmouth Camp in Wales and life was great. In late August they became regular soldiers and within weeks the British Army was mobilised when war was declared on 3 September 1939. After a brief leave at Christmas, Leslie reported to the R.A. depot at Wantage, Berkshire on 5 January 1940. From here he was sent to join the Honourable Artillery Company (H.A.C.) near London. Albert Tipping was posted to a shore battery near Plymouth.

Although enjoying army life, Leslie was frustrated with the lack of action and not being sent to France. Almost immediately, on arriving at the H.A.C. he was sent on leave for five days. Meeting Tipping while on leave he decided to spend an extra two days away and on his return to duty, Leslie found himself before his Commanding Officer charged with being nine days

AWOL (absent without leave). He appeared before a Court Martial, but because of his youth, he was given one month's military detention. While in Aldershot on detention, he came across the Irish Guards for the first time. The impression they made on him changed his life. In London, back in the H.A.C. he met a southern Irishman named Halloran who was one of many Irish contractors working there. Halloran invited Leslie to Glasgow to join the contract gang with the promise of providing him with a new ID card. Leslie became John Patrick Kenneally.

For whatever reasons, the lure of the Army drew him back. Under his new identity, John attended a recruiting office in Manchester and signed on with the Irish Guards. He was back in the Army within four weeks of his desertion. After a further four weeks training, he was posted to No. 1 Company of the Brigade of Guards – an undisputed crack battalion.

## North Africa

John's first action was in North Africa in the Medjerda Valley. His Company of Guards attacked at night on 23 April 1943, and despite being under heavy fire from German 88 mm guns, routed the enemy. Expecting a counter attack, the Guards dug in and on 25 April, Easter Monday, they waited for a dusk attack. They were expected to hold the position and control the valley and plains beyond.

John was unexpectedly called to see his Commanding Officer, Capt. Chesterton who said, 'Kenneally, I have a job for you.' With a radioman, he was instructed to crawl over the ridge of the hill and observe the enemy and report back to the Platoon Sergeant. This he undertook on 28 and 30 April. The *London Gazette* in August was to report the events that followed:

> On the 28th April 1943, the positions held by one Company of Irish Guards on the ridge … were about to be subjected to an attack by the enemy. Approximately one Company of the enemy were seen forming up preparatory to attack and Lance-Corporal Kenneally decided that this was the right moment to attack them himself. Single-handed he charged down the bare forward slope straight at the main enemy body firing his Bren gun from the hip as he did so. This outstanding act of gallantry and the dash with which it was executed completely unbalanced the enemy Company which broke up in disorder. Lance Corporal Kenneally then returned to the crest further to harass their retreat.
>
> Lance Corporal Kenneally repeated this remarkable exploit on the morning of the 30th April 1943 when, accompanied by a Sergeant of the Reconnaissance Corps, he again charged the enemy forming up for an assault. This time he so harassed the enemy, inflicting many casualties,

that this projected attack was frustrated; the enemy's strength was again about one Company. It was only when he was noticed hopping from one fire position to another further on the left, in order to support another Company, carrying his gun in one hand and supporting himself on a Guardsman with the other, that it was discovered he had been wounded. He refused to give up his Bren gun, claiming that he was the only one who understood that gun, and continued to fight all through that day with great courage, devotion to duty and disregard for his own safety.

Out of the 1st Battalion Irish Guards, just 80 survived these actions. A white marble cross now stands on the site to the memory of the commissioned officers, non commissioned officers and guardsmen who died there on 27-30 April 1943.

John's wound was under the right knee and he was sent to the casualty clearing station where basic first aid was administered to prevent the gangrene that so easily developed in the hot climate. Surgery later removed a 9 mm bullet from the wound.

Returning to Tunis where the 1st Irish Guards were bivouacked, he found a notice from General Alexander to Winston Churchill. Dated 10 May 1943 it stated, 'The Tunisia Campaign is over'.

During his interlude in North Africa, it was announced over the forces network news that King George VI had awarded him the Victoria Cross.

It is not known if the military establishment ever discovered that Kenneally was an army deserter in a former life, or what the reaction was if it did.

**Italy and the end of the war**
On 7 December 1943 the Battalion disembarked at Taranto, Italy and on 20 January 1944 re-embarked at Castellammare Bay to head for a landing at Anzio.

At 7:30 a.m. on 24 January the Brigade was given orders to advance in incessant bad weather. The battle was a bloody one and John was wounded in the wrist and out of the fighting for two weeks. The Battalion was at last relieved and taken out of Anzio. They landed in Liverpool on 22 April 1944 and were sent to Chelsea Barracks, London. The investiture of his medal was held in May 1944.

At the end of the war, John was posted to Germany and later signed for a further five years with the 1st Parachute Battalion with whom he was posted to Palestine, policing the area between Jews and Arabs. Later John purchased his discharge and his records state: Military Conduct: Very Good.

Nearly 40 years later John again met Capt. Chesterton at Wellington Barracks at the unveiling of the statue to Field Marshall Alexander.

## Retirement

In his later years, John resided in the village of Rochford where he died on 26 September 2000. He is buried in Rochford churchyard with the insignia of the 'Irish Guards' engraved on the headstone.

# Holly and Mistletoe

You wouldn't expect Tenbury to be the kissing capital of the world, but it just might be.

The Teme Valley has been full of orchards for centuries and old apple orchards are still happy sites for healthy clouds of mistletoe (

There are in fact 1,300 species of mistletoe, some of which are suitable for medical uses. In the past, mistletoe was used to treat many ailments from epilepsy to rheumatism. There is a theory that the word mistletoe originates from the Celtic word for 'all heal', and in years gone by folk medicine used it to treat what we now call high blood pressure and excessive cholesterol and as a diuretic. It also was felt to have a calming effect and so was used as treatment for epilepsy, hysteria, whooping cough and rapid heartbeat. Today active research is being undertaken to study its possible ability to destroy cancer cells, boost the immune system and protect DNA. Although the plant and berries are poisonous in their natural state, few side effects have been so far found in the extracts used in the research.

The hemiparasitic plant (i.e one that requires a host but is able to manufacture its own chlorophyll and to function as a normal green plant) has been collected and sold in the valley and to the local trade in Tenbury since time immemorial. However, these sales became more organised with the building of the Round Market, and the coming of the railway in 1862. Once larger market possibilities were available, wholesalers began to advertise locally for mistletoe and high quality holly to sell in the north and in London. As a result local farmers and gypsies gathered huge amounts and the seasonal sales became grand events.

There is a newspaper report dating from 1885 concerning Thomas Graves, a fruit merchant of 46 Teme Street, who sold one ton of holly and a half-ton of mistletoe to America. The holly and mistletoe were packed into sugar tierces for the trip. (A tierce is a large cask capable of holding about 42 gallons of wine.) In 1893 Chris Smith of Callow Hill, Worcestershire sent 10 cwt of mistletoe by train from Tenbury to Chesterfield. In 1919 The Worcestershire Fruit and Vegetable Society was prepared to pay 10s per cwt.

A specialised market in mistletoe and holly began with the involvement of auctioneers Edwards, Russell and Baldwin in 1924. Through various incarnations, these auctions have continued to the present day. Three markets are usually held at the end of November and beginning of December with the price of good quality mistletoe being in the region of £1 per lb. (Sales now also include Christmas wreaths and Christmas trees.) The most recent markets have welcomed greengrocers, flower merchants and wholesalers for the supermarkets from all over the British Isles and Europe.

Mistletoe has mystic and historic connections and has been associated with the Druids. Because it remained green throughout the winter it was felt to have special properties and was cut on the sixth day of the moon with a gold, silver or bronze sickle and divided among the people. Especially potent was the mistletoe cut from the oak tree which was hung over the doorway to ward off evil. Perhaps this is the origin of kissing under its leaves.

Holly on the other hand has connections with the Biblical crown of thorns and drops of blood, but its mythology is even older. Protection seems to be its strength and prickly boughs brought into a house prevented malevolent fairies from harming those who lived there, while providing a place for good fairies to shelter. Leaving holly trees uncut in a hedge was meant to prevent witches from running along the tops. Amazingly holly is said to provide protection from lightning and so it was often planted near houses. It is now known that the uniquely shaped holly leaves act as tiny lightning rods and so do provide protection for the tree and naturally the house as well.

*Holly and Mistletoe sale in the auctionyard in Tenbury in the 1980s*

*Holly and Mistletoe sale in the auctionyard in Tenbury in 2002*

With the decline of orchards in the Herefordshire, Worcestershire, Shropshire triangle there has been concern about the amount of mistletoe available. However it is found that mistletoe will also grow happily on poplar, lime, hawthorn, blackthorn, ash or rowan. It is planted by birds that wipe the sticky seeds onto branches, where with luck they will take root.

The well known holly and mistletoe auctions have continued to take place in the town, but with the sale of the auction yard in Tenbury and the uncertain future of the site, a committee of local people has begun celebration of these wonderful plants with an annual festival in early winter.

In 2005 Parliament declared 1 December to be National Mistletoe Day and on the weekend closest to this date the town of Tenbury holds a festival in celebration of this mystical plant. The Festival crowns a Mistletoe Queen and Druids are invited to bless the plant. Other events vary: there are concerts by well known artists, teas, art workshops, sales, a Mistletoe Ball and a short story writing competition.

For details about the Festival visit www.tenbury-mistletoe-festival.co.uk and come to Tenbury to join in the fun.

# Bibliography

Anon, *Hutchinson The Encyclopedia of Britain,* Helicon Publishing Ltd, 1999

Anon, *The Brief History of Hop Picking*, National Hop Association

Anon, unpublished collection of sketches and paintings by members of the Croquet Club

*Berrows Worcester Journal*

Bevis, Peter, *Historical Aspects*, the Tenbury Historical Society, 2001

Blackwell, A., *Historic Bridges of Shropshire*, Shropshire Libraries, 1985

Bond, Francis, *The Chancel of English Churches,* Humphrey Milford, OUP, London 1916

Chadwick, Eileen, *The Craft of Hand Spinning*, Batsford Ltd, London, 1980

Cooke, Ruth, 'The Other William Morris'*, Journal of Stained Glass*, Vol XXIV, British Society of Master Glass Painters, London, 2000

Evans, M.A., Howell T., *History of England and Wales, Vol II*, The Educational Publishing Co Ltd., Cardiff, 1910

Froggatt, Jim, *Jim Froggatt at Hillwood Farm*, unpublished notes, 1995

Gas Inspectors Minute Book 1877-1895

Griffin, Fanny, *22 Teme Street, Tenbury Wells, 1932*, unpublished notes, 1932

Guide to The Church of St Michaels & All Angels, Tenbury Wells.

Haig, Christopher (ed), *The Cambridge Historical Encyclopedia of Great Britain and Ireland,* Cambridge University Press, 1985

Hartland, R.A., *Jottings of the Early Days of the Tenbury Fire Brigade*, unpublished, 1987

Hey, David, *The Oxford Companion to Local and Family History*, Oxford Press, 1996

Hodder, M A., 'An Ice House in Sandwell Valley; Excavation and Restoration, 1982-3'*, Transactions of South Staffordshire Archaeological and Historical Society*, 1987.

Holding, Richard, *'The Song of the Watermill'* as quoted in *Down Along the Temeside,* Reliance Printing Works, 1979

Holt, Tonie & Valmai, *Battlefields of the First World War, A Traveller's Guide,* Pavilion Books Ltd., London, 1993.

Jenkins, A E, *Titterstone Clee Hills, Everyday Life Industrial History and Dialect*, pub by A.E. Jenkins, 1983

Jones, Lawrence E., *The Observer's Book of Old English Churches,* Frederick Warne & Co Ltd, London, 1965

Joyce, MA, F. Wayland, *Tenbury, Some Record of its History*, Oxford University Press, 1931

Kenneally, J.P., *Kenneally V.C.,* Kenwood, 1991

Lee, Lawrence, Seddon, George and Stephens, Francis *Stained Glass,* A H Artists House. London, 1982

Lewis, Malcolm J., 'Tower Captain St Mary's Tenbury', *Teme Valley Magazine,* Tenbury Wells Team Ministry, March 2006

Log Books of Tenbury National School

Miller, Howard, numerous files, papers, notebooks, photographs, maps, census records, reports and displays all unpublished

Miller, Howard, *Tenbury Wells and the Teme Valley, the Archive Photographs Series,* The Chalford Publishing Company, Stroud, 1996

Miller, Howard, *Tenbury Wells and the Teme Valley, The Second Selection, Images of England,* The Chalford Publishing Company, Stroud, 1998

Miller, Howard, *The Parish Church of Saint Mary,* Saint Mary's Church, Tenbury

Minutes of the Baptist Chapel

Minutes of the National School Committee

Morton, A.L, *A People's History of England,* Lawrence & Wishart, 1938 and 1999

Moxon, James, *The Forgotten Battle of Standard Oak,* undated, unpublished paper

Mrs Hewitt, Transcript of audio tape

Mytton, Geoff, Notes

Powis, Doug, untitled notes, unpublished, 1995

Spilsbury, E.H., Memoirs of Edwin Henry Spilsbury, unpublished notes

Tetsall, John, untitled notes, unpublished, undated

Tevelyan, G.M. *History of England,* Longmans, Green & Co. Ltd., London, 1942

The Hop Guide (NHA)

*The London Gazette*, Friday 13 August, 1943: Report of Tuesday 17 August, 1943

*The Tenbury Wells Advertiser*, various dates

Vince, John, *Discovering Watermills,* Shire Publications, Stroud, 1987

Wheeler, E.N. *Journey to France – September 1919,* unpublished notes, undated

*Worcester Postman* (later Berrows Worcester Journal) 1739

Young, Peter, letter to James Moxon, 1986 (copy in files)

## Websites

www.spartacus.schoolnet.co.uk/NORarchcanterbury.htm
www.william1.co.uk/w3.html
www.naval-military-press.com
www.victoriacross.org.uk
www.worcesternews.co.uk
http://archive.worcesternews.co.uk
www.tenbury-misteltoe-festival.co.uk

## Further reading available from Tenbury Library or booksellers

*History of Tenbury*, Tunstall Evans. May be read at Tenbury Library but not borrowed
*Innes and Publick Houses of Tenbury*, David Morrison and Howard Miller
*Tenbury and District in Wartime*, compiled by Howard Miller
*Tenbury Wells Pump Rooms, an illustrated history 1840 – 1938* by Howard Miller is available in the Pump Rooms
*The Tenbury and Bewdley Railway*, Keith Beddoes and William H Smith.
*Historical Aspects 1, 2 and 3*, Tenbury Historical Society. Book 3 is available from the Society

# Index

Numbers in italics refer to illustrations

Eliot, Rev. W.N.G.  80, 90
Elizabeth, Princess  6
Ertment, Ernie  *168*
Essex, Earl of  17
evacuated children  160
Evans, Sarah  38

Farmer, Private  142
Farr  *150*
    Dr  134
Faulkner, Felix  27
fever hospital  113, *179*
Field Farm  133, 170
field names  19
Field, Samuel  107
    William  107
Finch, William  27
fire, at Eastham Grange  98
    at Harp Bank, Burford  94
    at Kyrewood  *96*
Flax Farming  19 – 20
Fletcher, Volunteer  *148*
flood of 1770  12
    1886  75, 76
    1899  *77*
    1901  *78, 80*
    1910  *79, 80*
    1924  *77, 78*
Foley, Edward  117
Food and Drugs Act  31
Foresters Court  88
Foster, John  45
    Sarah  *23*, 45
Fox, Richard  46
Froggatt, James  27, 167, *167*, 171
    Tony  167
Fuller, Corporal  142
Fullers, Mr and Mrs  83
funeral hatchments  8

Gallows Bank  63
Garmsley  58
Gent, John  13
ghost, St Mary's Church  82
Giant of Burford  7
Gibbons, 'Golly'  *99*
Giles, Rev. George  88, 89
Ginridding  122
Godson, Gerald  *150*, 151 157, *157*
    Mr S.H.  69, 75, 82

Goff Schools  33, *34*, 44
Goff, Edward  33, 45
Goff's School Building  44, 45, *45*, 165
Goldingham, Lieutenant Colonel, H.  141
Golley, James  32
Gore Ouseley, Rev. Sir Frederick  53, 86, *86*, 90, 104
Gore, Samuel  30
Gothic Revival  53, 55
Grandfield, Hugh  30
Grandstand Cottage  103
Graves, Thomas  177
Greenhill, John  46
Greete  5, 172
Grey, Mr  35
Grice, Ernest  30
Griffin, Mrs Ann  75, 76, 79, 83
    Alfred  75, 76, 79, 82
    Elizabeth  76, 79
    Fanny  75 – 84, *76*
    George  75, 76, 77, 79, 80, 82, 83, 84
    John  75
Griffiths, Volunteers  *148*
Grove, T.  111
Guiness  *168*

Hall, Rev. George  38
Hamar Powis, Kath  170
Hampton, Rev. J.  90
Handley, Arthur  14
    Geoff  *168*
    Mr  75
Hanley Mill  117
Hanley William  117
Hardemann, Mr  97
Hardman, John and Company  53, 54, 55
Hare, Thomas  38
Harp Bank, Burford, fire at  94
Hartland  *150*
    Charlie  *168*
    Jr W.  98
    R.A.  91
    W.  94
harvest  119
Hay, Fred  *168*
Haynes, John, DS  26, *27*, 27, *28*, 29, 30, 31, 32
Henges, Jane  81, 82
Heritage, Alfred  45
Hernaman, Rev.  43

191